MW00681510

DAVID ORTIZ presents

COOKING WITH THE PROS

New England Sports Edition, Volume I

PICTURED: CHRIS HOGAN'S MAKE IT SPICY MEATBALLS!

Cooking with the Pros: New England Sports Edition (Volume I)

Benefiting the

DAVID ORTIZ
Children's Fund

Created by: Susan Mulcahy
Lead photographer: Dave Harding
Design by: Daniel Guidera
Special Thanks to: David and Tiffany Ortiz

Photography:
Daryl Adams
Matt Burrows
Jeff (JR) Ramsey
Susan Mulcahy

Copy editor: Margaret Mulcahy
Editorial assistant: Kirsten Hunter

Additional photos:
Rod Mar, Russ Mezikofsky, Chandrashiv Pandoo, Natalie Lynn

A NOTE FROM BIG PAPI

DAVID ORTIZ Children's Fund

"*I love kids and being able to help those in need through my Fund is something that gives me and my family so much gratification and I'm just so appreciative to be in a position to be able to help. With this cookbook we hope to continue our mission. I would personally like to thank all of the athletes and their families that helped make this cookbook a reality. It is through the generous giving of their time that we will be able to continue to make a difference. I hope everyone enjoys this cookbook as much as my family and I do.*"

–DAVID ORTIZ

ABOUT THE DAVID ORTIZ CHILDREN'S FUND

Founded by David and his wife Tiffany, The David Ortiz Children's Fund is committed to helping children in New England and the Dominican Republic who do not have access to the critical pediatric services they need. They are proud to partner with Massachusetts General Hospital for Children and World Pediatric Project through its work with CEDIMAT to fulfill their goals.

"*The Fund is just such a special way that David can use his celebrity to bring so much joy and happiness to the kids we are able to help. We've always instilled in our own children how important it is to be kind and caring people and they get to see us really lead by example when it comes to our works with The Fund. It makes us all more humble and aware of how fortunate we are, and how we have the ability to positively impact other children and family's lives in so many ways.*" *–Tiffany Ortiz*

Working together with projects like this cookbook, The Fund is increasing the number of children receiving lifesaving surgeries. To date, they have netted more than $2 million for children in need and saved over 600 lives in the Dominican Republic and helped countless others in the New England area.

This cookbook is dedicated to my Mother, Angela Rosa Arias.

With love, David

CREATOR
SUSAN MULCAHY

For my brother Tommy, The greatest Red S fan ever.

Love, Susan

LEAD PHOTOGRAPHER
DAVE HARDING

@DAVEISMEDIA

In loving memory of Milt Schmidt

"Mr. Bruin"

1918-2017

INTRODUCTION

Welcome to "Cooking with the Pros", the New England Sports Edition. This cookbook has been a labor of love for myself and my team. For as long as I can remember, I have had a passion for sports both as a participant and a spectator. We are so fortunate to live in the greatest part of the country for sports, New England. Our region has the best teams, players, coaches, owners and last but certainly not least, fans. And what goes along hand in hand with our favorite sporting events? Well, food, of course.

In this edition of "Cooking with the Pros", we are taking you inside the lives of our beloved athletes and sports figures, as they share their favorite recipes and let us in on the stories and secrets behind their dishes. The participants graciously donated their time and their kitchens for one of the most important causes there is, helping children.

We are thrilled to partner with David and Tiffany Ortiz and The David Ortiz Children's Fund on this incredible cookbook. Proceeds from your generous purchase of this cookbook will go directly to The Fund. Their sole mission is to assist children in the Dominican Republic and New England who are in need of life saving surgeries.

So while you think about the incredible things these athletes and sports figures have achieved while competing, I also ask you to think about what amazing human beings they are to participate in this effort. Whether they are or were Red Sox, Patriots, Bruins, Celtics or Olympians, they are all humanitarians who came together for a purpose.

My profound thanks to everyone who participated and to all the fans and chefs out there, happy cooking!

–Susan Mulcahy

A Channel Media Production

Copyright© 2017 by Channel Media.

All rights reserved, including all rights to reproduction.

Printed by: LSC Communications

Printed in: USA First Edition: December 2017

Library of Congress Cataloging In-Publication Data:

Mulcahy, Susan, Cooking with the Pros, The New England Sports Edition

Photography by: Dave Harding, Daryl Adams, Matt Burrows, Jeff Ramsey and Susan Mulcahy

ISBN: 978-0-692-81640-0

UPC: 8683020000407

Additional Photo/Image Credits:

Alamy, AP Images, Getty Images, Megapixl, Rueters, Cleveland Indians

SPECIAL THANKS TO

Hallie Lorber and The David Ortiz Children's Fund

Boston Red Sox

New England Patriots

Boston Bruins

Boston Celtics

New England Revolution

ESPN

Arias Wines

Brett Petersen, ACME Sports

ABC Creators

Jill Leone

Reagan Communications

Acapulcos (Sudbury, MA)

Bozzuto

Boston Children's Hospital Trust

grown™

Rich Ansara, Tresca (Boston, MA)

Susan Hurley & Charity Teams LLC

Tom McCarthy & TPM Progressive Sports

Frank Bailey, Beth Emery & Boston College

Kim Ward & Twin River Casino (Lincoln, RI)

Chill Kitchen & Bar (Marlboro, MA)

Charlie Moore Productions

Erin Lynch & FM Productions

Radegen

Goodwin Public Relations

Snapfish

Brian Mik, University of Hartford

The Ritz-Carlton New York

Swymfit

Renaissance Inn at Patriot Place

John Caron & West End Johnnies

Anne Wilcox & Doubleback Wines

Deco's Italian Cuisine

Kim Fauria, KJ Designs

Karen Wonoski & Boston Bruins Alumni Association

Todd Civin & Civin Media Relations

Lincoln Tavern & Restaurant (South Boston, MA)

K Sports and Entertainment

Curtis Danburg & The Cleveland Indians

Saratoga Food & Wine Festival

Roche Brothers/Sudbury Farms

Catania Oils

Eddie Rhodman, Jr., Destined for Success Management

Flutie's Sports Pub (Plainville, MA)

SSG Football

Big Papi's Kitchen

PICTURED: THE COCHRAN FAMILY'S BEST EVER CAKE

Table of Contents

Breakfast/Snacks... 13

Lunch.. 33

Appetizers... 67

Sides.. 89

Main Courses... 119

Desserts.. 199

Index.. 219

PICTURED: HANNAH KEARNEY'S COTTAGE CHEESE PANCAKES

Breakfast & Snacks

ANDREW FERENCE'S
Frozen Acai Bowl

INGREDIENTS

2	frozen **Sambazon Acai** *packages*
1	*banana*
1	*package frozen* **pineapple**
1	*package frozen* **mango**
2	*tablespoons* **Manitoba Harvest Hemp Hearts (Seeds)**
½	*cup* **granola**
2	*tablespoons* **honey**
1	*cup* **almond milk**
	a good **blender**

(Note: For this recipe you can substitute any frozen fruit and ripe fruit you would like— strawberries, peaches, cherries, raspberries, etc.)

Place the frozen mango and pineapple (or chosen fruit) in a blender with the frozen acai, almond milk liquid (about a ¼ cup) and blend until combined.

Keep adding the liquid as needed to get a frozen gelato style consistency (make sure the mixture stays thick).

Place in a bowl and add granola, hemp hearts, sliced bananas and drizzle with honey.

MAKES **4** SERVINGS

> "*What I like about this recipe is you can vary it in so many ways. You can make it with all types of fruit, substitute juice for the almond milk and sprinkle all kinds of good things on the top. My kids love it because they think they're getting a treat but it's incredibly healthy. It's important to start children with a healthy foundation so that they continue to make smart choices.*"
>
> **—ANDREW FERENCE, BOSTON BRUINS 2007-2012**

ANDY IS DEDICATED TO ASSISTING TEAMS AND BUSINESSES BE MORE SUSTAINABLE AND MAKE BETTER ENVIRONMENTAL CHOICES. HE LEADS THIS MOVEMENT BY EXAMPLE BY BEING AS ECO-FRIENDLY AS POSSIBLE IN HIS PERSONAL LIFE AND CREATING PROGRAMS SUCH AS THE CARBON-NEUTRAL PROGRAM FOR THE NHL, WHICH TRIES TO EFFECTIVELY COUNTERACT THE NEGATIVE IMPACT OF PROFESSIONAL SPORTS BY ALLOWING PLAYERS TO PURCHASE CARBON OFFSET CREDITS.

—@FERNUCKLE

DON MCKENNEY'S
Asparagus and Egg Tart

INGREDIENTS

6	*eggs*
1	cup *milk*
2	cups *Gruyere cheese* (shredded)
1½	pounds medium thick *asparagus* (ends trimmed)
1	tablespoon *olive oil*
2	teaspoons *pepper*
2	teaspoons *salt*
1	sheet *puff pastry*
1	tablespoon *flour*
1	tablespoon *butter*
1	*lemon*

MAKES 8 SERVINGS

> **"This asparagus and egg tart is very tasty and is good for a breakfast, lunch or brunch. Over the years we think it tastes best cooking the asparagus a little bit first. This allows everything to come out at the same time cooked perfectly and ready to eat."**
>
> **–DON MCKENNEY
> BOSTON BRUINS 1954-1963**

 Preheat the oven to 400°.

 In a bowl mix the eggs, milk, pepper and salt until combined and set aside.

 Lightly butter and flour the bottom of a 9 by 12 inch baking pan. Roll out the puff pastry into the baking pan and press gently to even it out. Make sure the puff pastry covers the entire pan and press slightly around the sides.

 Using a fork, score the puff pastry around the pan, brush with olive oil.

 Pour the egg mixture into the baking pan and spread the cheese over the top. Place in the oven for 12 minutes.

 While the egg mixture is cooking, cook the asparagus in a quart of boiling water for 5 to 7 minutes.

 Drain the water and squeeze the juice of one lemon over the asparagus (this will allow it to keep its green color).

 Remove the baking pan from the oven and place the asparagus crosswise over the egg mixture. (Be careful as the pan will be hot).

 When the entire pan is covered with the asparagus, place the pan back into the oven for 35 minutes.

 Let stand for 5 to 10 minutes before serving.

JARROD HAS BEEN AN ATHLETE ALL HIS LIFE, GROWING UP PLAYING BASEBALL, SOCCER AND ANY OTHER SPORT HE COULD TRY. HE FELL INTO DOING TRIATHLONS AFTER RUNNING IN COLLEGE. JARROD IS PASSIONATE ABOUT BEING OUTDOORS AND ENCOURAGING PEOPLE TO BE PHYSICALLY FIT AND STAY ACTIVE

—@JARRODSHOEMAKER

JARROD SHOEMAKER'S
Banana Bread

INGREDIENTS

1½   cups **flour**

1½   cups **sugar** (*or for a healthier alternative use **3/4 cup sugar** and **3/4 cup applesauce***)

1   teaspoon **baking soda**

⅛   teaspoon **salt**

½   cup **butter**

½   cup **buttermilk**
    (*or regular milk with a dash of **vinegar***)

2   **eggs**

1   teaspoon **vanilla**

½   cup **nuts** of your choice
    (**walnuts** or **pecans** work best)

3   large **bananas**

1   cup of **chocolate chips**

MAKES  SERVINGS

☯ Preheat the oven to 375°.

☯ Grease and flour two loaf pans.

☯ Using a mixer on low, mix together the flour, sugar, baking soda, salt, butter, buttermilk, eggs and vanilla together until you get a smooth batter.

☯ Add the bananas and mix on low until you get your desired consistency.

☯ Stir in the chocolate chips and the nuts until thoroughly combined and pour half into each loaf pan.

☯ Bake for 35 to 40 minutes (A deeper loaf pan might take a bit longer and a shallow pan might take a bit less).

☯ To test if it is done use a knife or toothpick and put into the banana bread (If anything sticks when you pull it out it is not done yet).

☯ Let sit for 10 to 15 minutes before eating and enjoy!

> "Being a triathlete I love cooking and eating. I have traveled around the world and I love tasting local cuisine, but nothing compares to home cooked banana bread. I end up eating it for dessert and breakfast!"
>
> –JARROD SHOEMAKER, OLYMPIC TRIATHLETE, 2009 ITU DUATHLON WORLD CHAMPION
> HOMETOWN: SUDBURY, MA

"After 13 years on the U.S. Ski Team and 3 Olympic appearances, I retired in 2015. I lived in Vermont for 29 years, but moved to Utah after retiring to attend Westminster College. I love to hike and bike with my dog Finn while listening to my favorite podcasts. My professional future after graduating is still uncertain, but I do know that it will include cottage cheese pancakes!"

—HANNAH

HANNAH KEARNEY'S
Cottage Cheese Pancakes

INGREDIENTS

2   cups **cottage cheese** *(we used 2%)*

4   **eggs** *(lightly beaten)*

½   cup **wheat flour** *(substitute **white flour, coconut flour, banana flour** if desired)*

1   tablespoon **butter** *(melted)*

    Salt

MAKES **2-3** **SERVINGS**

Combine all the ingredients together in a bowl

Melt the butter on a hot skillet.

Once melted and very hot, ladle the batter on the skillet in a circular motion.

Cook each pancake and flip when brown.

Note: You can serve the pancakes with fruit, honey, and/or Vermont maple syrup (as shown here).

> "I like cottage cheese pancakes because they are simple, high in protein and surprisingly delicious. I eat them for breakfast, lunch, or dinner and I add some Vermont maple syrup if I am craving something sweet. I got the recipe from my aunt when I visited her in Nova Scotia and I made them for my teammates when I was training and competing. To this day, they send me photos whenever they whip up a batch."

–HANNAH KEARNEY, OLYMPIC MOGUL SKIER
GOLD MEDAL 2010, BRONZE MEDAL 2014
HOMETOWN: NORWICH, VT

MILT SCHMIDT'S
Easy Breakfast

INGREDIENTS

2 eggs

3 slices **Canadian bacon**

½ can **baked beans**

1 tablespoon **butter**

1 teaspoon **pepper**

MAKES **1** SERVING

- Using a large skillet, heat the butter over medium heat until melted.

- On one side of the skillet pour in the baked beans and heat for 2 minutes.

- Add the Canadian bacon and cook for 3 minutes.

- Flip over the bacon and drop in the eggs.

- Cook until the eggs are at your desired consistency (about 3 minutes) and sprinkle with pepper.

- Serve immediately.

> "While I've never been much of a cook, when I was asked to do this I thought 'does opening a can count?' However, I do make some simple things like this easy breakfast."
>
> **—MILT SCHMIDT**
> **BOSTON BRUINS 1936-1942, 1945-1955, HALL OF FAME 1961**

JAY HEAPS'
"The Thing that Rises"

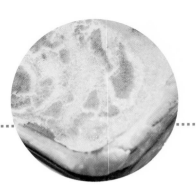

INGREDIENTS

4	tablespoons **butter**
1	cup **flour**
6	large **eggs**
1	cup **milk**
1	teaspoon **salt**
2	tablespoons **cinnamon sugar**
	Maple syrup

MAKES 4-6 SERVINGS

⚽ Preheat the oven to 425°.

⚽ Once oven is warm place the butter into an 8 by 13 inch glass baking dish and place in the oven until the butter is melted (about 2 minutes).

⚽ Spread the melted butter over the bottom of the dish.

⚽ In a medium bowl, mix the flour, eggs, milk and salt. Stir all the ingredients together until completely mixed and pour into the baking dish.

⚽ Sprinkle the cinnamon sugar over entire top of the mixture and place in the oven.

⚽ Bake for about 15 to 18 minutes or until the edges are cooked and mixture has risen.

⚽ Serve immediately with maple syrup.

> "When I was a kid my mom would make this recipe on the weekends and special occasions. We never knew the true name of it so we just called it 'The Thing That Rises'. It's sort of a combination of a pancake and French toast. Now, my kids love it and we are passing down this tradition to the next generation."
>
> **–JAY HEAPS, NEW ENGLAND REVOLUTION, PLAYER 2001-2009, COACH 2011-2017 HOMETOWN: LONGMEADOW, MA**

"I was extremely close with my mother, as a family we had so many great traditions. My Mom passed away a number of years ago. She was a recipient of a lung transplant and died a year later. I feel so blessed to have had her for that year and I am a big advocate for organ donation, it really can change so many lives."

—JAY
WWW.ORGANDONER.ORG

"Years ago, I handed my son and daughter who were getting ready for a track meet, a bag of homemade trail mix. I said, 'If you want to fly like a bird, you've got to eat like a bird'—here's a bag of nuts, seeds, and berries—this stuff will make you fly! It's still true today."

—KAREN GILLESPIE
(GIRLFRIEND OF BILL RODGERS)
WWW.BILLRODGERSRUNNINGCENTER.COM

BILL RODGERS'
Spiced Pecans

INGREDIENTS

2	tablespoons **unsalted butter**
3	tablespoons **chili powder**
1½	teaspoons **salt** (preferably **sea salt**)
¾	teaspoon **Cayenne pepper**
½	teaspoon **cumin**
1	pound **pecans** (**almonds** can be substituted)

MAKES  **SERVINGS**

👟 Preheat the oven to 350°.

👟 Melt the butter in skillet on low and stir in pecans.

👟 Add all the seasonings and mix well (about 2 minutes).

👟 Transfer to a baking dish or cookie sheet.

👟 Bake 15 to 20 minutes.

👟 Check after 15 minutes to prevent burning.

> *"As an athlete, what you put into your body is very, very important. These nuts taste great and they are a great source of protein and healthy fats, two things that are key to the success of all athletes, especially runners."*
>
> **–BILL RODGERS, FOUR-TIME BOSTON MARATHON WINNER**
> **HOMETOWN: HARTFORD, CT**

JARVIS GREEN'S
Spicy Cornbread

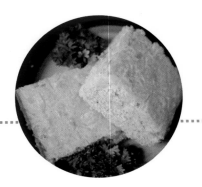

INGREDIENTS

1½   cups **corn meal**

1   cups **flour**

2½   cups **sugar**

2   teaspoons **baking soda**

1   teaspoon **salt**

2   cups **butter**

1⅓   cups **milk**

2½   cups shredded **cheddar cheese**

4.5   ounce can **green chilies peppers** (drained)

4   **eggs**

- Preheat the oven to 375°.

- Grease and flour two loaf pans.

- Using a mixer on low, mix together all the ingredients until you get a smooth batter.

- Mix in the jalapenos and stir until combined.

- Pour half of the mixture into each loaf pan.

- Bake for 35 to 40 minutes (A deeper loaf pan might take a bit longer and a shallow pan might take a bit less).

- Let sit for 5 to 10 minutes and serve

MAKES 12 SERVINGS

“*What I like about this cornbread is that you can eat it alone or with a main meal. It's even a nice substitute for rice or potatoes.*”

**–JARVIS GREEN
NEW ENGLAND PATRIOTS, 2002-2009**

"I grew up with my Mom, grandma and aunties all teaching me how to cook. Now my three kids love to eat, so we cook a lot. I like dishes that are savory, wholesome and that feed the whole family."

—JARVIS
@JARVISGREEN97

TOM WERNER'S
Roasted Chestnuts

INGREDIENTS

1½ to 2 pounds **chestnuts**

> **"**One of my fondest early memories growing up in New York City was buying roasted chestnuts in Central Park. On a brisk fall day, it was wonderful comfort food and far better health wise than a boiled hot dog.**"**
>
> **– TOM**

MAKES (3-4) SERVINGS

⚾ Preheat the oven to 425°

⚾ In a saucepan, mix the cornstarch into the cream (on very low heat), just bring the saucepan to a simmer and add 2 tablespoons of the sour cream and the cheese. Stir until the mixture is smooth.

⚾ With a sharp paring knife, score an X on the rounded side of each chestnut. Make sure to break through the shell but avoid cutting too deep into the nut.

⚾ Place the chestnuts in a pot and cover them with cold water and bring them to a boil over high heat. Drain and immediately transfer them to a foiled, shallow baking pan and arrange them in a single layer, flat side down.

⚾ Bake in the oven (on the middle rack) for 15 to 20 minutes until the shells have peeled back and the chestnuts are golden brown in color.

⚾ Wrap the hot chestnuts in a tea towel and squeeze them to loosen the shells. Let them sit for 5 to 6 minutes.

⚾ Peel the shells while they are still warm and enjoy!

> **"**These chestnuts are perfect for a cold New England afternoon. The good news is that this recipe is extremely easy to follow. The bad news is that chestnuts are really only available between September through December but this recipe tastes and smells delicious.**"**
>
> **–TOM WERNER, BOSTON RED SOX CHAIRMAN 2001-PRESENT**

PICTURED: TIM WAKEFIELD'S LOBSTER GRILLED CHEESE

Lunch

SIMON SHNAPIR'S
Russian Borscht

INGREDIENTS

- **10** ounces **red beets** (grated on a ¼ inch grater)
- **10** ounces **green cabbage** (sliced into strips)
- **1** large **carrot** (grated)
- **2** medium **white potatoes** (cubed)
- **1** medium **white onion** (minced)
- **1** clove **garlic** (minced)
- **2** tablespoons **tomato paste**
- **1** **lemon** (de-seeded)
- **1** teaspoon **sugar**
- **2** tablespoons **Parsley** (chopped)
- **1** tablespoon **dill** (chopped)
- **½** cup **sour cream**
- **Salt**
- **Pepper**

MAKES 4 SERVINGS

IIn a stock pot, bring 2.6 quarts of water to boil over medium-high heat. Stir in the potatoes and cook for 10 minutes.

Add the cabbage and continue cooking for 7-10 minutes until both cabbage and potatoes are fork tender. Season with salt and pepper (to taste) and set aside.

In a large pan heat 1 tablespoon of olive oil. Add the onion and garlic, and cook for 2 to 3 minutes until golden and fragrant. Add the carrots and beets and sauté for 5 to 7 minutes stirring frequently. Simmer the vegetables for 15 to 20 minutes. Stir in tomato paste, 2/3 cup of water and season with salt and pepper (to taste).

To the soup pot add the sautéed vegetables, sugar, juice of a quarter lemon, cover and simmer on low heat for 5 minutes. Test the soup and add salt and pepper (if needed, to taste).

Garnish bowls with fresh parsley, dill and a dollop of sour cream.

Serve with warm crusty bread.

> **"Borscht is a traditional Russian and Ukrainian soup which my grandmother [pictured] has made for me for many years. I like it because it's comforting and healthy. The beets give this dish its traditional red color and it can be made with meat too but I like this lighter version for lunch."**
>
> **–SIMON SHNAPIR, OLYMPIC PAIRS FIGURE SKATER, BRONZE MEDALIST 2014
> HOMETOWN: SUDBURY, MA**

SIMON WAS BORN IN RUSSIA AND MOVED WITH HIS FAMILY TO MASSACHUSETTS WHEN HE WAS 16 MONTHS OLD. IN 2015, HE RETIRED FROM PAIRS SKATING COMPETITION. HE IS NOW THE HIGH PERFORMANCE DIRECTOR AT THE SKATING CLUB OF BOSTON.

"I learn as much from them as they learn from me."

—SIMON
@SIMONSHNAPIR

STEVE GROGAN'S
Calico Bean Casserole

INGREDIENTS

6	slices of **bacon**
1-2	pounds of **hamburger** (substitute ground **turkey** or **chicken**, if desired)
1	medium **onion** (chopped)
½	cup **catsup**
½	cup **light brown sugar**
2	tablespoons **vinegar**
2	tablespoons **mustard**
1	can **lima beans** (drained)
1	large can **pork and beans**
1	can **kidney beans**

MAKES 6-8 SERVINGS

🏈 In electric skillet cook the bacon and drain.

🏈 Once the bacon is cool, chop into small pieces and set aside.

🏈 In the same electric skillet sauté the onion over medium high heat for 3 to 4 minutes.

🏈 Add the hamburger until brown (about 5 minutes).

🏈 Add the ketchup, vinegar, mustard, brown sugar, lima beans, kidney beans and pork and beans to the skillet and cook on low for 10 to 15 minutes.

🏈 Pour in the chopped bacon and cook for another 5 minutes.

🏈 Serve immediately.

🏈 Note: This recipe can be made using various types of canned beans.

> **"What I like about this recipe is it even tastes better the next day. It's a great recipe for freezing and having meals later. You could also use it as a filling for stuffed peppers or for a dip with tortilla chips and shredded cheese."**
>
> **–STEVE GROGAN, NEW ENGLAND PATRIOTS 1975-1990**

STEVE STILL LIVES IN NEW
ENGLAND AND KEEPS BUSY
WITH HIS BUSINESS GROGAN-
MARCIANO SPORTING GOODS
AND IS EXTREMELY ACTIVE
WITH THE EASTER SEALS.

"*They [the Easter Seals]
do so much to help
children and adults, it's
an honor to get to be a
part of it.*"

—STEVE
WWW.EASTERSEALS.COM/MA

JOSH IS ONE OF THE FOUNDING PARTNERS (ALONG WITH A NUMBER OF OTHER FORMER MAJOR LEAGUE PLAYERS) OF HOMEPLATE PEANUT BUTTER. HOMEPLATE IS MADE FROM NATURAL AND SUSTAINABLE INGREDIENTS AND CAN NOW BE FOUND IN THE CLUBHOUSE OF ALL 30 MAJOR LEAGUE TEAMS.

"It's just a wholesome great tasting peanut butter."

–JOSH
(HOMEPLATEPB.COM)

JOSH BECKETT'S
Kicked Up Peanut Butter & Jelly

INGREDIENTS

8   slices of **bread** *(your choice)*

1   jar of **grape jelly**

1   jar of **peanut butter**
     (we used HomePlate)

3   **eggs**

1   cup of **milk**

1   teaspoon **vanilla**

1   teaspoon **cinnamon**

MAKES (4) **SERVINGS**

⚾ In a bowl mix the eggs, milk, vanilla and cinnamon.

⚾ Spread the peanut butter on four slices of the bread and the jelly on the four other slices.

⚾ Press one slice of the peanut butter and one slice of the jelly together in a sandwich and make four sandwiches.

⚾ Dip each side of the sandwiches into the egg mixture and make sure both sides are coated.

⚾ On a grill pan over medium-high heat place the sandwiches and cook for 3 minutes then flip and cook the other side for another 3 minutes.

⚾ Serve immediately.

> **"I really like something simple sometimes like a peanut butter and jelly sandwich. This one is a little kicked-up but still has the same flavors that everyone likes."**
>
> **–JOSH BECKETT**
> **BOSTON RED SOX 2006-2012**

VINNY PAZ'S
Protein Packed Lunch

INGREDIENTS

2	6 ounce packets **tuna** or **salmon** (no drain variety)
⅓	cup **blueberries**
1½	tablespoons **olive oil**
¼	cup ground **walnuts**
¼	cup sliced **almonds**
2	teaspoons of **vinegar**
2	tablespoons **parmesan cheese**
2	small **pita pockets** (or **6 Ritz crackers**, optional)

🥊 Combine the tuna or salmon in a bowl with the olive oil and vinegar and stir together.

🥊 Add the walnuts, almonds and blueberries and stir until all the ingredients are combined.

🥊 Sprinkle the parmesan cheese into the bowl and mix by hand to desired consistency.

🥊 Serve in a pita pocket or with crackers (if desired).

MAKES 2 SERVINGS

> **"This recipe is quick, loaded with protein and makes an incredibly healthy lunch or snack. It's something that I ate in my fighting days and I continue to eat now to stay in shape. If you're in a rush you can actually cut this recipe in half and make it right in the pouch."**
>
> **—VINNY PAZ, 5 TIME WORLD CHAMPION BOXER**
> **HOMETOWN: CRANSTON, RI**

"*I've lived in other places but being a New Englander is very important to me. That's why I've always felt like Rhode Island is my home. We have the greatest sports teams, players and fans in the world here.*"

—VINNY
@5XPAZ

SCOTTY LAGO'S
Venison Chili

INGREDIENTS

2   tablespoons **cooking oil**
2   pounds **ground venison**
      (substitute **beef** or **turkey** if desired)
2   large **garlic cloves** (minced)
28   ounces **crushed tomatoes**
      (substitute **fire roasted** if desired)
2   tablespoons **chili powder**
1   teaspoon **cumin**
1   teaspoon dried **oregano**
1   teaspoon **cayenne pepper**
1   teaspoon **onion powder**
1-2   teaspoons **red chili flakes**
      (depending on how spicy you like it)
3   tablespoons **brown sugar**
½   teaspoon **cayenne**
1   teaspoon **salt**
½   teaspoon fresh **cracked pepper**
¼   cup **corn flower**
1   16-ounce can **pinto beans**
      (drained and rinsed)
1   16-ounce can **kidney beans**
      (drained and rinsed)

MAKES 6-8 SERVINGS

◎◎◎ Place the oil, ground venison and garlic in a large pot. Cook over medium heat until the meat is browned.

◎◎◎ Pour in the tomato sauce, chili powder, cumin, oregano, salt, onion powder, red chili flakes, brown sugar, pepper and cayenne.

◎◎◎ Stir together well, cover and then reduce the heat to low. Simmer for 45 minutes to 1 hour, stirring occasionally.

◎◎◎ In a small bowl, mix the corn flour with ½ cup of water to create a paste. Pour the paste into the chili and mix well.

◎◎◎ Taste test the chili to see if you need to add any more spices or corn flour paste.

◎◎◎ Add the pinto and kidney beans into the chili. Simmer for an additional 5 minutes.

◎◎◎ Serve with any of your favorite toppings: shredded cheese, red onions, tortilla chips, cilantro, hot sauce or lime wedges.

> "What I like about this is I can make this ahead of time and keep it in the fridge so I always have something filling on hand to grab. Venison is also one of the healthiest meats out there, high protein, low in fat and I harvest my own deer every year so I know where the meat is coming from."
>
> —SCOTTY LAGO, OLYMPIC SNOWBOARDER, BRONZE MEDAL 2010
> HOMETOWN: SEABROOK, NH

SCOTT NOW SPENDS HIS TIME TOURING DOING AIR SHOWS AND IS CONCENTRATING ON HIS LAGO SNOWBOARD LINE.

"*I just love being in New England, all my friends and family are here. I could never see leaving this area, it is home.*"

—SCOTTY
@SCOTTYLAGO

TIM IS CURRENTLY ON NESN AS A STUDIO ANALYST FOR THE BOSTON RED SOX. HE IS ALSO EXTREMELY INVOLVED IN CHARITABLE CAUSES BOTH IN FLORIDA AND NEW ENGLAND AND IS THE HONORARY CHAIRMAN OF THE RED SOX FOUNDATION.

"*I'm always happy to participate in causes that I am passionate about.*"

—TIM
@TIMWAKEFIELD49

TIM WAKEFIELD'S
Lobster Grilled Cheese

INGREDIENTS

1   *pound **lobster salad** (or **lobster meat**)*

1   *cup **spinach** or **kale***

1   ***tomato** (sliced)*

¼   *pound of **cheese** (sliced, your choice)*

4   *slices of **bread** (your choice)*

2   *tablespoons **mayonnaise***

MAKES **2** **SERVINGS**

To build each sandwich, place the greens on one slice of the bread, add the cheese, then the lobster and finally the tomato slices and top with another piece of bread.

Spread the mayonnaise on both outer sides of each sandwich (this will allow it to brown when cooking and give the sandwich excellent flavor).

In a fry pan on medium heat, place each sandwich and cook each side for 3 minutes.

Let sit for 2 to 3 minutes, cut in half and serve.

> "*Lobster salad always makes me think of New England and it's such a big part of the culture here. This sandwich is a little different than the average lobster roll and has great flavor—enjoy!*"
>
> **–TIM WAKEFIELD**
> **BOSTON RED SOX 1995-2011**

DAVE COWENS'
Miso Udon Noodle Soup

INGREDIENTS

2	tablespoons **sesame oil**
1	tablespoon **ginger** *(minced)*
1	tablespoon **garlic** *(minced)*
4	ounces **shitake mushrooms** *(sliced thin)*
2	cups **carrots** *(sliced thin)*
2	cups **baby kale**
1	package firm **tofu**
2	tablespoons **miso paste**
6	cups **chicken broth**
2	packages **udon noodles**
1	cup **snow peas** *(sliced}*
2	tablespoons **scallions** *(sliced)*
1	tablespoon of **soy sauce**

MAKES 3-4 SERVINGS

> **"I never really wanted a big meal before a game. I prefer something that is hearty, healthy and doesn't make me feel weighed down. This soup is something I like because it's healthy and satisfying and a good source of protein."**
>
> **–DAVE COWENS**
> **BOSTON CELTICS 1970-1980**
> **HALL OF FAME 1991**

✱ Remove the tofu from pack and drain. Wrap it in a paper towel and soak up extra moisture and slice into 1 inch cubes.

✱ In a large sauté pan, heat 1 tablespoon of sesame oil until hot. Add the tofu slices to sauté pan in one single even layer (working in batches if needed). Sear for 3 to 4 minutes on each side, or until golden brown. Remove from heat and set aside.

✱ Heat oil in large pot over medium high heat, add the garlic and ginger and sauté for 1-2 minutes.

✱ Add the mushrooms and carrots to pot and sauté for an additional 5 minutes. Add the baby kale and stir until wilted.

✱ While the kale is cooking, measure miso paste into a small bowl. Add ¼ cup of the chicken broth and mix well.

✱ Once kale is wilted, add the miso/chicken broth mixture to pan and stir. Slowly add the remaining chicken broth and bring to a boil.

✱ For a thicker soup: Once the water is boiling, add the udon noodles and cook for 7 to 8 minutes or until noodles are cooked through. For a thinner soup: Fill a separate pot with water and bring to a boil. Add the udon noodles to boiling water and cook for 7 to 8 minutes. Drain the noodles and add to soup separately.

✱ Once noodles are cooking in the soup OR added to the soup, add sliced snow peas.

✱ Serve noodles in a bowl and garnish with scallions and drizzle with soy sauce.

"*Being a chef in a school system I get to see first-hand how important it is to instill good eating habits in young children. It's extremely important to get kids to try new food items and experiment with recipes. If they have healthy food preferences now, they will make good dietary choices for the rest of their lives.*"

—SAMANTHA COWENS-GASBARRO

MAX LANE'S
Taco Goulash and Frito Salad

INGREDIENTS

For the taco goulash

1	package **taco seasoning**
2	pounds **ground beef**
1	package **macaroni and cheese sauce** (any type with the cheese sauce in a squeeze pouch)
1	cup spicy **tomato juice**
1	cup **yellow onion** (chopped)

For the Frito salad

1	package **salad mix**
1	cup **Italian dressing**
1	cup **Fritos**

MAKES 6 **SERVINGS**

🏈 In a skillet over medium-high heat brown the hamburger (about 7 to 10 minutes) and add the taco seasoning (set aside).

🏈 In a large pot bring 2 quarts of water to boil. Add the macaroni until cooked (about 10 to 12 minutes). Drain the macaroni and place back in the pot.

🏈 Add the hamburger, tomato juice and cheese and stir over medium heat until all ingredients are combined. Cook for another 5 minutes on medium heat while continuing to stir.

🏈 Serve with the Frito salad.

🏈 For the Frito salad: In a bowl mix the salad mix and the Fritos. Once mixed, add the Italian dressing and let sit until the dressing is fully absorbed into the Fritos (add additional dressing if desired).

> **"This is a recipe I learned from my Mom years ago and whenever I go home she always makes it for me. Now, I make this for my own kids all the time. It's easy and they like it, which is important being a single dad. I typically serve it with my sister's Frito salad. Something about the salad, dressing and the crunch of the Fritos, give it a great taste."**
>
> **–MAX LANE, NEW ENGLAND PATRIOTS 1994-2000**

MAX IS EXTREMELY INVOLVED IN THE LOCAL COMMUNITY. HE IS ACTIVE WITH CHARITABLE ORGANIZATIONS AND IS A VOLUNTEER COACH FOR HIS SON'S HIGH SCHOOL FOOTBALL TEAM. MAX IS A COMMERCIAL REAL ESTATE AND INSURANCE CONSULTANT AND IS THE NFL UNIFORM INSPECTOR FOR THE NEW ENGLAND PATRIOTS.

"It's a great way to still stay connected with the game."

—MAX

DAVID ORTIZ'S
Chicken Quesadilla

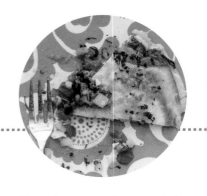

INGREDIENTS

2	large **tortillas**	
¼	cup **yellow onions** (chopped)	
¼	cup **chicken** (cooked, chopped)	
¼	cup **shredded cheddar cheese**	
¼	cup **green pepper** (chopped)	
½	cup **salsa**	
	(we used **Big Papi's** Kitchen	
	Black Bean and Corn Salsa)	
1	tablespoon **olive oil**	

MAKES (1-2) SERVINGS

⚾ Lay one of the tortillas down and spread the onion, chicken, cheese and green pepper evenly. Place the remaining tortilla over the top.

⚾ In a large skillet, heat the olive oil over medium heat for 2 minutes. Place the quesadilla in the pan and cook for 8 minutes (flip after 4 minutes).

⚾ Cut the quesadilla into slices, smother with salsa

"*This recipe is very easy to make and does not take a long time to cook. You can use different ingredients and customize it to your taste. It tastes better if you eat this quesadilla while it's warm.*"

—DAVID ORTIZ
BOSTON RED SOX 2003-2016

DAVID'S WIFE TIFFANY IS DEDICATED TO CAUSES EVERYWHERE THAT AFFECT CHILDREN. SHE IS THE CO-FOUNDER OF THE DAVID ORTIZ CHILDREN'S FUND AND COMMITTED TO THE FUND'S MISSION.

"*We never want to see a child who needs surgery turned away over lack of funds.*"

—TIFFANY ORTIZ
@TIFFANYORTIZ4
DAVIDORTIZCHILDRENSFUND.ORG

ERIN PAC'S
Pulled Pork Tacos

INGREDIENTS

For the tacos

5 *pound* **pork butt**

10-12 *medium* **flour tortillas**

For the slaw

⅓ *cup* **white vinegar**

⅓ *cup* **extra virgin olive oil**

2 *tablespoons* **white sugar**

3 **limes** *(juice only)*

1½ *cups* **red cabbage** *(thinly sliced)*

1½ *cups* **green cabbage** *(thinly sliced)*

2 **jalapenos** *(chopped) (optional)*

½ *cup* **carrots** *(shredded)*

½ **red bell pepper** *(thinly sliced)*

½ **yellow bell pepper** *(thinly sliced)*

½ *cup* **cilantro** *(roughly chopped)*

½ **purple onion** *(thinly sliced)*

Salt

Pepper

For the tomatillo avocado salsa

6-8 *medium* **tomatillos**

3 *ripe* **avocados**

2 **garlic cloves** *peeled*

2 **limes** *(juice only)*

½ *cup of* **cilantro**

Salt

⚬⚬⚬ In a crock pot place the pork butt for 8 to 10 hours with desired seasoning until tender and shred with a fork.

⚬⚬⚬ In a bowl, mix together all ingredients for the slaw and salt and pepper (to taste).

⚬⚬⚬ Combine all the ingredients for the tomatillo avocado salsa in a bowl and blend until smooth.

⚬⚬⚬ To assemble, warm up tortillas on skillet and add as much pork and slaw as you want.

⚬⚬⚬ Top with salsa and serve.

MAKES **6** **SERVINGS**

> ❝**This recipe is one of my favorites, it's colorful and incorporates so many healthy ingredients. It's great for lunch, dinner or even a snack.**❞
>
> **–ERIN PAC BLUMERT**
> **OLYMPIC BOBSLEDDER**
> **BRONZE MEDAL 2010**

TOM CARON'S
Southwest Lasagna

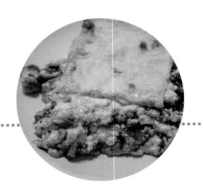

INGREDIENTS

1   pound **ground beef**

1   small **onion** (chopped)

¼   teaspoon **garlic powder**

1   package **taco seasoning**

16   ounces of plain **tomato sauce**

1   cup **cottage cheese**

1   cup **sour cream**

4   ounces **green chili peppers** (deseeded, finely chopped)

1   package medium **flour tortillas**

8   ounces shredded **sharp cheddar**

MAKES 4-6 SERVINGS

Preheat the oven to 375°.

In a frypan add the ground beef, taco seasoning, 1 tablespoon of onion and brown over medium-high heat (about 7 to 8 minutes).

Drain thoroughly add the tomato sauce and garlic powder and set aside.

In a bowl combine the cottage cheese, sour cream, chili peppers and stir together.

Using an 8x8 inch baking pan start building the layers. First place 2 tortillas in the baking dish (covering the bottom). Add a layer of the beef mixture, a layer of the cottage cheese mixture and a layer of the cheese.

Repeat the exact same process for the second layer. Cover with two tortillas for the top.

Place in a 375° oven for 45 to 50 minutes. Let cool for 10 minutes and enjoy.

> *"My wife and I really like southwest style food. This is easy to make and is a great dish to bring to a tailgate or someone's house. It can be served with other dishes or just a simple salad. You can put your own twist to it by using ground turkey or chicken and adding salsa."*
>
> —TOM CARON, BOSTON RED SOX SPORTSCASTER, NESN ANCHOR
> HOMETOWN: LEWISTON, ME

"*I'm a local guy who grew up in Maine and come from an entire family of very hard working people. I, on the other hand, am blessed with being able to sit around and talk baseball all day and have 23 years at NESN. My first year as studio host for the Boston Red Sox they won the World Series (in 2004). I am so grateful to love what I do.*"

—TOM
@TOMCARON

JERMAINE WIGGINS
Wiggy's Chicken Parm Subs

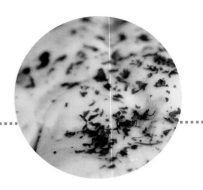

INGREDIENTS

4   **chicken cutlets** *(sliced thin)*

1   **egg**

1   jar **tomato sauce** *(your choice)*

2   tablespoons **breadcrumbs**

2   tablespoons grated **parmesan cheese**

1   tablespoon **olive oil**

2   tablespoons chopped **parsley**

4-8   slices **provolone cheese**

4   small/medium **sub rolls**

MAKES **4** **SERVINGS**

- Preheat the oven to 350°.

- In a small bowl quickly whisk the egg. With a basting brush coat the chicken cutlets with the egg.

- In a bowl, combine the parmesan cheese, breadcrumbs and 1 tablespoon of the chopped parsley. Dip each side of the chicken cutlets into the mixture.

- In a skillet, heat the olive oil (about 2 minutes) and sauté the chicken cutlets over medium-high heat for 4 minutes (2 minutes on each side).

- Place the chicken into a baking pan, cover with the tomato sauce and bake for 10 to 12 minutes. Add a slice of cheese on the top of each cutlet and place back in the oven for 2 to 4 minutes (until the cheese is melted).

- Garnish with remaining parsley and place each cutlet into a sub roll (you can also toast the roll), and enjoy!

> **"I grew up on Italian food and I love it! Actually everyone loves chicken parmesan. It's easy and my wife makes it a lot for me and the kids. What I like to do with this is make it extra cheesy by adding another slice of cheese to the roll."**
>
> **–JERMAINE WIGGINS**
> **NEW ENGLAND PATRIOTS 2000-2002, HOMETOWN: EAST BOSTON, MA**

JERMAINE STILL RESIDES IN NEW ENGLAND AND IS CURRENTLY A RADIO HOST FOR HOT 96.9'S MORNING SHOW, HAS HIS OWN PODCAST AND IS A SOUGHT AFTER TELEVISION PERSONALITY. HE IS ACTIVE IN LOCAL CHARITIES BUT FOR HIM IT'S ALL ABOUT FAMILY.

"At the end of the day what matters most to me is my wife and kids."

—JERMAINE
@JWIGGS85

MATT CHATHAM'S
Colorado Green Chili

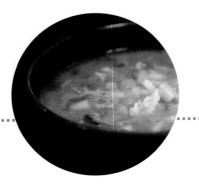

INGREDIENTS

1½	pound	**pork roast**
2	tablespoons	**olive oil**
50	ounces	**chicken broth**
2-3	cups	**water**
1	medium yellow sweet	**onion** (chopped)
1	glove	**garlic** (chopped)
2		**poblano chilies** (chopped)
2	medium	**tomatillos** (chopped)
2		**serrano chilies** (chopped)
8	ounces	**stewed tomatoes**, with juice
4	cans	**green chilies** (chopped)
1		**habanero chili pepper** (chopped)
3	links	**chorizo** (cut into ¼' inch pieces)
1	tablespoon ground	**cumin**
¼	teaspoon	**oregano**
¼	teaspoon	**cayenne pepper**
½	cup	**flour**
1	tablespoon	**honey** (if needed)

MAKES (10) SERVINGS

In a deep pot, heat the olive oil on medium heat and sear pork on all sides. Add half of the broth and 1 cup of water and bring to a boil. Lower the temperature to simmer and cook until pork falls apart (approximately 3 hours).

In a skillet sauté the onion, garlic, and poblano peppers in olive oil (about 3 minutes). Add the chorizo and brown (about 3 minutes).

When the pork is done, shred pork in the liquid it was cooked in.

Slowly add in all the ingredients (except for flour, water and honey) and bring to a boil. Reduce the heat and simmer for at least an hour.

In a separate (closed) container, mix flour and 1 cup of water, shake well (100 shakes recommended).

Add the flour and water mixture to the chili and stir (if the chili is too thick slowly add water to achieve desired thickness). If the chili is too spicy, add some of the honey to cut the flavor and sweeten.

Garnish with sour cream, tortilla chips, scallions and salsa (if desired).

> "Having spent a lot of time in Colorado, I like the green type of chili instead of the bean style. This chili has some heat to it but it's very hearty. You can eat it in a bowl or you can use it as more of a dip with tortillas or chips. It's something I love to make. I usually double the recipe and freeze half for later."
>
> –MATT CHATHAM, NEW ENGLAND PATRIOTS 2000-2005

MATT AND HIS WIFE ERIN STILL RESIDE IN NEW ENGLAND. HE IS AN ANALYST FOR NESN AND SHE IS BUSY WORKING FOR THE JOE ANDRUZZI FOUNDATION. THE FOUNDATION IS DEDICATED TO PROVIDING HELP, HOPE, AND A REASON TO SMILE BY CONTRIBUTING FINANCIAL ASSISTANCE TO CANCER PATIENTS AND THEIR FAMILIES WHEN IT IS NEEDED MOST.

"*We are aiming to relieve the cancer financial burden by paying for things like rent, electricity, heat, etc., so patients and their families can focus on recovery, not bills.*"

—ERIN CHATHAM @ERINCHATHAM, @CHATHAM58, JOEANDRUZZIFOUNDATION.ORG

RICKY CRAVEN'S
Fish Chowder

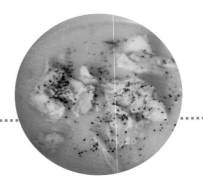

INGREDIENTS

10	slices **bacon** *(cut into small pieces)*
2	**yellow onions** *(sliced thin)*
4	pounds **haddock** *or* **cod filets** *(skin removed)*
1	stick **butter**
6	**Yukon gold potatoes** *(peeled and cubed)*
½	cup **Sherry cooking wine**
1	quart **half and half**
1	teaspoon **Tabasco sauce**
2	cups **water** *or* **broth**
2	tablespoons **olive oil**
	Salt
	Pepper

MAKES 8 SERVINGS

In a stock pot (or Dutch oven) heat the olive oil and sauté the bacon and onion on medium heat until the onions are translucent (about 5 minutes). Be careful not to caramelize the onions.

Add the potatoes, water or broth and salt and pepper (to taste) and let simmer for 20 minutes until the potatoes start to become soft.

Place the fish on top of the mixture and add the Tabasco sauce, sherry cooking wine and salt and pepper (to taste). Simmer for 15 minutes (you should start to see the fish fall apart).

Add the half and half and the butter. Allow to simmer an additional 40 to 45 minutes, stirring occasionally.

Shut the stove off and allow the chowder to sit for 45 minutes (this will allow the flavors to combine together).

When you are ready to serve, heat the chowder back up over medium heat for 10 minutes.

> **"This fish chowder recipe is a twist on one my father-in-law used to make. It's really something we enjoy on special occasions or holidays. The chowder actually tastes best if you refrigerate it overnight and then heat it up the next day, so you can always make it ahead of time."**
> —RICKY CRAVEN, NASCAR DRIVER HOMETOWN: NEWBURGH, ME

RICKY CURRENTLY WORKS FOR ESPN AS NASCAR ANALYST. HE CURRENTLY DIVIDES HIS TIME BETWEEN NORTH CAROLINA, CONNECTICUT AND MAINE.

"*Along with my passion for racing, I just love New England and feel the most at home in Maine. There's just so much to do here all year round.*"

—RICKY
@RICKYCRAVENESPN

TITO'S PASSION FOR ITALIAN
FOOD, NORTHEAST OHIO AND
CHARITY HAS LEAD HIM AND
HIS FATHER TO TEAM UP OFF
THE FIELD TO CREATE TITO
FRANCONA AND SONS PASTA
SAUCE. PROCEEDS FROM THE
SALES OF THE SAUCE WILL
BENEFIT THE CLEVELAND
INDIANS CHARITIES.

*"I try to do as much
locally as possible."*

—TERRY
(FRANCONAPASTASAUCE.COM)

TERRY FRANCONA
Francona Family Meatballs

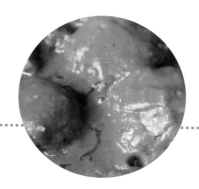

INGREDIENTS

2	tablespoons **olive oil**
1	pound **ground beef** (85% lean)
½	pound **ground pork**
½	pound **ground veal**
½	cup **whole milk**
2	cups day-old **Italian bread** cubed
2	large **eggs**
3	large cloves **garlic** (minced)
¼	cup flat leaf **parsley** (finely chopped)
¾	cup grated **Parmesan cheese**
2	24 ounce jars **Tito Francona and Sons Marinara Sauce** (or sauce of choice)
1	teaspoon **pepper**
1	teaspoon **salt**

MAKES 4 SERVINGS

> **"I had a love of Italian food growing up, it always reminds me of family. These meatballs are very tender and flavorful. The key is to not overcook them, they should just be at the point where they break apart easily."**
>
> **–TERRY FRANCONA, BOSTON RED SOX MANAGER 2004-2011**

⚾ In a bowl add the bread and milk. Let the bread soak in the milk, mix thoroughly.

⚾ Squeeze the milk out of the bread, drain and then mash the bread. Set aside any of the remaining milk to add to the meat mixture later.

⚾ Place about a third of each of the meats in large mixing bowl.

⚾ Add the garlic, parsley, drained bread, salt and pepper.

⚾ Mix with your hands until completely combined.

⚾ Add the rest of the meat, remaining milk, eggs and cheese.

⚾ Gently combine the ingredients thoroughly but be careful not to beat or over work the mixture. The object is to produce light meatballs that are easily breakable.

⚾ Form meat into plum size balls. Add olive oil to a large fry pan and gently sauté meatballs on all sides until light brown on all sides (about 10 minutes). (Do not brown to a dark crust otherwise meatballs will be too tough).

⚾ Add the tomato sauce to the pan and finish cooking the meatballs (about 10 minutes).

⚾ Garnish with parsley and grated cheese (if desired).

LONIE IS NOW THE HEAD OF GLOBAL MARKETING AT GOPRO. THE COMPANY MANUFACTURES AND SELLS CAMERAS FOR ACTION SPORTS AND DEVELOPS ITS OWN MOBILE APPS AND VIDEO EDITING SOFTWARE.

"I like being a part of working with this incredible technology developed by our amazing creative team."

—LONIE
@LONIEPAXTON
@GOPRO, GOPRO.COM

LONIE PAXTON
Have It Your Way Stromboli

INGREDIENTS

2	10 ounce packages **pizza dough** (or you can make your own)
1	pound **salami**
1	pound **sliced turkey**
1	pound **cheese slices** (your choice)
½	cup **red peppers** (diced)
½	cup **green peppers** (diced)
½	cup **yellow peppers** (diced)
½	cup **yellow onion** (diced)
1	cup organic brown sugar
2	large **tomatoes** (sliced)
1	tablespoon **olive oil**

MAKES **6-8** SERVINGS

🏈 Preheat the oven to 400°.

🏈 Lay out the pizza dough on a floured surface and roll until both pieces measure roughly 12x10 inches. Place one slice on a cookie sheet.

🏈 Start layering the dough; first with the salami, then the turkey, then the cheese and finally the tomato slices. Sprinkle the peppers and the onions evenly over the top.

🏈 Place the other piece of pizza dough over the top. Fold the dough over and pinch the ends and sides together all the way around.

🏈 Pierce the top with a sharp knife three or four times. Brush the top with the olive oil.

🏈 Bake in the oven for 15 to 20 minutes, slice and enjoy.

> "What I like about this recipe is that you can make it with anything you want. You can select all different cold cuts, cheeses and vegetables. It's a great recipe to do with the family and get the kids involved."
>
> —LONIE PAXTON
> NEW ENGLAND PATRIOTS 2000-2008

PICTURED: DAVID ORTIZ'S BEEF EMPANADAS

Appetizers

JONNY HAS SERVED AS A COLOR ANALYST FOR THE BOSTON RED SOX. HE IS KNOWN FOR HIS CHARITABLE EFFORTS NOT ONLY IN FLORIDA WHERE HE LIVES BUT ANYWHERE THERE IS A CAUSE CLOSE TO HIS HEART. IN 2017, HE FORMED THE JONNY GOMES 707 RELIEF FUND TO ASSIST PEOPLE WHO WERE AFFECTED BY THE WILDFIRES IN CALIFORNIA.

"I grew up playing ball there and I want to help them rebuild."

— JONNY
@JONNYGOMES5

JONNY GOMES
It's not Nachos, It's Gomes

INGREDIENTS

2	tablespoons **butter**	
2½	cups **corn** (fresh or frozen)	
½	cup **black beans**	
2	tablespoons **green pepper** (chopped)	
2	tablespoons **red pepper** (chopped)	
1	tablespoon **yellow onions** (chopped)	
4	tablespoons **mayonnaise**	
1	tablespoon **cornstarch**	
¾	cup **heavy cream**	
1	cup shredded **Monterey Jack cheese**	
1	bag **tortilla chips** (your choice)	
¼	cup **feta cheese crumbles**	
4	tablespoons **sour cream**	
1	tablespoons **cilantro** (chopped)	
	Cayenne pepper (to taste)	
2	**limes** (cut into wedges)	

MAKES 6 **SERVINGS**

☺ In a large skillet, melt the butter over medium high-heat, add the corn and cook until it starts to get a char on it (about 6 to 7 minutes), add the black beans, red pepper, green pepper and onions: cook until all the vegetables get a good char on them (5 to 6 minutes).

☺ Once the vegetable mix is at your desired consistency, add the mayonnaise. Stir until the mayonnaise is combined and set aside.

☺ In a saucepan, mix the cornstarch into the cream (on very low heat), just bring the saucepan to a simmer and add 2 tablespoons of the sour cream and the cheese. Stir until the mixture is smooth.

☺ Place the tortilla chips on a tray, pour the cheese mixture over the top then add the corn mixture. Sprinkle the top with the feta, cilantro and cayenne (to taste).

☺ Squeeze the juice of a couple of the lime wedges over the top and garnish with remaining limes and sour cream (if desired).

> **"This nacho recipe is vegetarian but extremely tasty. It's simple to make but the flavors go awesome together. You can add as much heat as you want to it."**
> **–JONNY GOMES, BOSTON RED SOX 2013-2014**

RAY BOURQUE
Anna Maria's Baked Stuffed Meatballs

INGREDIENTS

For the meatballs

2	pounds **ground chuck**
1	pound **ground veal**
3	**eggs**
4	ounces grated **grana parmesan cheese**
4	ounces shredded **cheddar cheese**
2	ounces whole **onion** *(pureed and drained)*
2	tablespoons **Italian parsley** *(finely chopped)*
1	tablespoon **dry oregano**
1	teaspoon **black pepper**
1	tablespoon **salt**
1	tablespoon granulated **garlic**
1	cup fine **Italian breadcrumbs**
1	cup pureed **marinara sauce**
2	ounces **Worcestershire sauce**
2	tablespoons **olive oil**

For the stuffing

16-20	**Ciliegine mozzarella** *(cherry size)*
4	ounces **Cipollini onions** *(chopped)*
4	ounces roasted **red** or **yellow peppers** *(chopped)*

MAKES (2-4) SERVINGS

- Preheat the oven to 350°.
- Soak the breadcrumbs in the marinara puree for 5 minutes.
- In a large mixing bowl add the ground chuck, ground veal, eggs, parmesan cheese, cheddar cheese, onion, parsley, oregano, black pepper, salt, garlic, and Worcestershire sauce. Mix ingredients together by hand until combined.
- Add the soaked breadcrumbs and continue to mix by hand until all ingredients are blended well.
- Apply a bit of olive oil to your hand and start rolling the meatball mixture into 4 ounce balls.
- After all the meatballs have been rolled, make an indentation with your thumb about halfway in to individually stuff each meatball.
- Place one mozzarella ball into the indentation followed by a pinch of the onions and then a pinch of the roasted peppers. Push the stuffing halfway in and close the meatball by pinching the meat together and rolling until smooth. Repeat for the remaining meatballs.
- Place the meatballs on a cookie sheet (sprayed with cooking spray) and bake in the oven for 20 minutes.
- Serve hot with your favorite tomato sauce and grilled crusty bread.

> "*This dish we serve as an appetizer at our restaurant Tresca. It is named for a woman named Anna Maria who visited Tresca and asked Rich (Rich Ansara, head chef of Tresca) to make her something really authentic and special. He came up with this and it is now one of our more popular items.*"
>
> **—RAY BOURQUE, BOSTON BRUINS 1979-2000, HALL OF FAME 2004**

IN ADDITION TO OWNING TRESCA, RAY IS VERY INVOLVED IN THE COMMUNITY AND NUMEROUS CHARITABLE CAUSES. HE HAS CREATED THE BOURQUE FAMILY FOUNDATION WHICH IS FOCUSED ON MAKING SURE FAMILIES EVERYWHERE HAVE ACCESS TO LIGHT, WATER AND SHELTER.

"*It's something I strongly believe in and is extremely special to me because my entire family is involved with it.*"

—RAY
@RAYBOURQUE77,
@BOURQUEFAMILYFOUNDATION,
THEBOURQUEFAMILYFOUNDATION.ORG

"Food has been such a big part of my culture, which is one of the reasons I have my own line of chips and salsa. I'm passionate about sharing some of the flavors I love."

—DAVID
(BIGPAPISKITCHEN.COM)

DAVID ORTIZ'S
Beef Empanadas

INGREDIENTS

1	large **yellow onion** (chopped)
1	package mild **taco seasoning**
1½	cups frozen **green peas**
1	pound **ground beef**
1	teaspoon **Adobo seasoning**
1	tablespoon **olive oil**
1	sheet **puff pastry**
1	tablespoon **flour**
1	**egg**
2	cups *Big Papi's Kitchen Salsa*

MAKES 4 SERVINGS

> **"These empanadas are filled with flavor and can be made using many different ingredients. You can use left overs, other meats and vegetables— have some fun and be creative. I love these covered in salsa."**
>
> **–DAVID ORTIZ**
> **BOSTON RED SOX 2003-2016**

☺ In a large fry pan heat the olive oil and sauté the onions over medium-high heat for 2 to 3 minutes.

☹ Lower the heat to medium, add the ground beef until the beef is brown (about 6 to 7 minutes).

☺ Then add the taco and Adobo seasonings and stir all the ingredients together.

☹ Once all the ingredients are combined, stir in the peas and cook for another 3 to 4 minutes and set the mixture aside to cool.

☺ Preheat the oven to 350°.

☺ On a lightly floured board roll out the puff pastry until you create an even oblong shape.

☹ Cut the puff pastry in half and then again on the diagonal.

☹ In a small bowl beat the egg.

☹ Place some of the mixture on each piece of the pastry and crimp the edges with a fork to seal.

☺ Place on a cookie sheet and lightly brush the top with the egg.

☹ Cook for 30 minutes and let cool for 10 minutes. Serve with salsa.

FROM 1979 TO 1987 JON WAS THE COLOR COMMENTATOR FOR THE NEW ENGLAND PATRIOTS RADIO BROADCASTS. HE NOW RESIDES IN SOUTH CAROLINA WITH HIS WIFE GAIL WHERE HE IS ACTIVE IN POLITICS AND AN AVID GOLFER.

"I have the most incredible memories of my playing days in New England."

—JON

JON MORRIS'
Spanish Dip

INGREDIENTS

½ cup **sugar**

½ cup **grape seed oil**

½ cup **apple cider vinegar**

1 can **black beans** *(rinsed and drained)*

1 can **pinto beans** *(rinsed and drained)*

1 can **white shoepeg corn** *(drained)*

1 can diced roasted **tomatoes** *(drained)*

1 small **red onion** *(chopped)*

1 large **green pepper** *(chopped)*

MAKES 8 SERVINGS

Using a saucepan, bring sugar, grape seed oil and apple cider vinegar to a slow boil stirring constantly until sugar is completely dissolved.

Remove from heat and cool.

In a bowl mix the black beans, pinto beans, corn, tomatoes, onion and pepper.

Stir gently until all the ingredients are combined.

Once the liquid has cooled, pour it over the beans mixture.

Refrigerate until serving.

Serve with scoop tortilla chips.

> "I like this recipe because it always tastes fresh and light. You can dip the tortilla chips into it or you could eat it with a salad or as a side. You can change it up by using other types of beans and vegetables."
>
> **–JON MORRIS**
> **NEW ENGLAND PATRIOTS 1964-1974, HOLY CROSS 1960-1964**

ALONG WITH PARENTS GORDY AND DIANE, BROTHERS GORDIE JR, DAN, CHRIS, ROB AND GLEN ARE ALL PART OF THE GRONK NATION YOUTH FOUNDATION. THE FOUNDATION'S MISSION IS TO INSPIRE YOUTH TO REACH THEIR FULL POTENTIAL THROUGH SPORTS, EDUCATION AND FITNESS. THEIR FAMILY MOTTO IS #GETYOURMINDRIGHT. FIND OUT HOW TO GET INVOLVED AT WWW.GRONKNATION.COM.

ROB GRONKOWSKI
The Gronkowski Family's Buffalo Chicken Dip

INGREDIENTS

12-14   ounces **chicken breast**

8   ounces **cream cheese**

1   15 ounce jar **Rootie's** or **Marie's Blue Cheese dressing**

½   cup **hot sauce** (we used **Frank's RedHot**)

🏈 In a baking dish cook the chicken breast thoroughly (350° for about 30 minutes). Make sure the chicken cools completely.

🏈 Once cool, shred the chicken using a grater that creates medium-size ribbons (set aside).

🏈 Over low heat, place the cream cheese in a saucepan until it softens, stirring occasionally. Be careful to keep the heat low so you don't burn the cheese.

🏈 Stir in the blue cheese dip until combined. Slowly add the hot sauce and shredded chicken and mix well together.

🏈 This dip can be served warm or cold. Serve with tortilla chips.

MAKES 8 SERVINGS

> **"Our Mom has made this dip for every tailgate we've had since we were children. As you can imagine, our family has done a lot of tailgating over the years."**
> **–ROB GRONKOWSKI, NEW ENGLAND PATRIOTS 2010-PRESENT**

DAN KOPPEN'S
Sweet and Savory Kielbasa

INGREDIENTS

1	cup dark **brown sugar**
1	cup **ketchup**
1	cup **yellow** or **Dijon mustard**
1	tablespoon **Worcestershire sauce**
1½	pounds **kielbasa** (cut into ½ inch pieces)

MAKES **4** **SERVINGS**

🏈 In a large zip lock bag add the brown sugar, ketchup, mustard, and Worcestershire sauce.

🏈 Close the bag and shake it or mix it up using your hand (on the outside of the bag).

🏈 Once the ingredients are combined, add the kielbasa pieces. Make sure the marinade covers all the kielbasa pieces evenly. Let this marinate for at least two hours or overnight.

🏈 When ready to cook, place all the kielbasa on a hot grill. Cook each piece for approximately 2 minutes per side (you should start to see a good char on the kielbasa).

🏈 Serve as an appetizer or on the bread or rolls of your choice.

> **"What I like about this recipe is that it's so easy but is a good blend of sweet and savory. This is great for a tailgate or a cookout because you can do so many things with it."**
>
> **–DAN KOPPEN**
> **NEW ENGLAND PATRIOTS 2003-2011, BOSTON COLLEGE 1999-2003**

DAN STILL LIVES IN NEW ENGLAND AND IS A FOOTBALL ANALYST FOR THE LOCAL NBC SPORTS NETWORK. HE IS ALSO A MOTIVATIONAL SPEAKER, A VOLUNTEER IN THE COMMUNITY AND A BUSY FATHER OF THREE CHILDREN.

"I love being involved and motivating people."

—DAN @KOPPEN67

ALONG WITH HIS MANY CHARITABLE EFFORTS, KEVIN IS THE OWNER OF LOMA
BREWING COMPANY (LOS GATOS, CA).

"*Aubree (Aubree Arndt, head chef) and I want to give people a
positive experience by having them try some interesting craft
beers and good food.*"

—KEVIN
@KYOUK_2036, LOMABREW.COM

KEVIN YOUKILIS'
Oktoberfest Mussels

INGREDIENTS

For the mussels

1	teaspoon **olive oil**
1	pound **PEI mussels** *(cleaned, remove beards)*
¼	cup **Oktoberfest beer** *(with 1 tablespoon extra to finish dish)*
¾	cup **clam juice**
1 ¼	teaspoons **lemon juice**
10	each **orange supremes** *(peel and segment orange, cut skin away from segment)*
1	medium **green onion** *(thinly sliced)*
1	tablespoon **unsalted butter**
1 ½	teaspoons **salt**
1	**lemon** *(for granish)*
	pinch **red chili flakes**

For the fennel confit

2	heads **fennel** *(core and slice fennel ¼ inch thick)*
4	cloves **garlic**
½	**lemon**
1	teaspoon **salt**

MAKES 8-12 SERVINGS

> **"This is a recipe we serve in my restaurant, Loma Brewing Company. The flavors go great together and it's a nice light appetizer. It's one of my favorites."**
>
> **–KEVIN YOUKILIS, BOSTON RED SOX 2004-2012**

☺ Preheat the oven to 350°.

☺ Lay fennel slices in oven proof pot, add the garlic, half of lemon and salt to pot. Cover the mixture with the olive oil.

☺ Wrap in aluminum foil and bake for about 30 minutes on 350F or until fennel is just soft.

☺ Note: This can be made days in advance, store in the oil to preserve and refrigerate until ready to use.

☺ Throw away any mussels that do not close when tapped on table or with spoon (they are dead).

☺ Heat up a large skillet on high until hot (about 2 minutes). Turn down the heat to medium and add the oil, mussels, and 1 teaspoon of salt. Toss the mussels until they start to open.

☺ Add strained fennel confit and garlic (remove the lemon half), clam juice, ¼ cup beer and lemon juice.

☺ Wait for mussels to open and add butter, orange supremes, green onion, and red chili flakes. Stir until the butter melts.

☺ Re-season with remaining beer, salt, and lemon juice.

☺ Garnish with lemon and serve with crispy buttered bread (if desired).

ROGER CLEMENS HAS SPENT TIME WORKING WITH NUMEROUS CHARITABLE ORGANIZATIONS. CLOSE TO HIS HEART IS THE ROGER CLEMENS FOUNDATION, AN ENTITY ENTIRELY DEDICATED TO HELPING CHILDREN. FOUNDED IN 1992 BY ROGER AND HIS WIFE DEBBIE, THE ORGANIZATION RAISES FUNDS THROUGH GOLF TOURNAMENTS, SILENT AUCTIONS AND OTHER EVENTS, FOR THE PURPOSE OF CARRYING ON AND SUPPORTING EDUCATIONAL, CHARITABLE, LITERARY, SCIENTIFIC AND RELIGIOUS ACTIVITIES FOR KIDS.

—WWW.ROGERCLEMENSFOUNDATION.ORG

ROGER CLEMENS
The Rocket's Swedish-Style Meatballs

INGREDIENTS

For the meatballs

½   pound ground **turkey**

½   pound bulk sweet **Italian sausage**

¼   cup **yellow onion** *(finely chopped)*

2   tablespoons dry **bread crumbs**

2   drops **hot pepper sauce**

1   **egg** *(lightly beaten)*

1   tablespoon **olive oil**

For the sauce

1   cup **water**

1   tablespoon of **flour**

1   tablespoon **ketchup**

1   teaspoon **Worcestershire sauce**

¾   teaspoon **beef flavor bouillon**

½   teaspoon **dried oregano**

½   teaspoon **black pepper**

¼   cup **sour cream**

MAKES  SERVINGS

⚾ In a large bowl, combine all the meatball ingredients (except the olive oil). Mix well and then shape into 40 1-inch balls.

⚾ Heat oil in a large skillet over medium-high heat and then add the meatballs and cook until brown (about 7 to 10 minutes).

⚾ Drain and return the meatballs to the skillet.

⚾ In a small saucepan combine all sauce ingredients (except the sour cream). Blend everything well with a wire whisk.

⚾ Cook over medium heat stirring often until the mixture thickens and boils.

⚾ Pour the sauce over the meatballs and simmer on low for 10 minutes. Slowly stir in the sour cream and cook an additional 3 to 5 minutes (until heated through).

⚾ Serve on a tray or transfer to a crock pot to keep them warm. Serve with toothpicks.

> **"This is a favorite in our household. You can always double or triple the recipe during the holidays or for a larger crowd."**
>
> **–ROGER CLEMENS, BOSTON RED SOX 1984-1996**

TED JOHNSON
Junior's Nachos

INGREDIENTS

1	pound **brisket**
1	bottle **BBQ sauce** *(we used the* **Original Rib Tickler** *restaurant's sauce)*
8	ounces **smoked garlic sausage** *(cut into ¼" pieces)*
2	cups shredded **extra sharp cheddar cheese**
15	ounces **ranch style beans** *(or* **Boston Baked Beans***)*
2	medium size **tomatoes** *(diced)*
1	cup **scallions** *(diced)*
1	package **tortilla chips**
⅓	cup **cilantro** *(chopped)*
¼	cup **sour cream**
2	**jalapenos peppers** *diced*
¼	cup **salsa** *(we used* **Big Papi's Kitchen Salsa***)*

MAKES 6-8 SERVINGS

For the slow cooked brisket

🏈 Place the brisket in a slow cooker, add the BBQ sauce of your choice and cook on low for 8 to 10 hours (you can also cook the brisket in a smoker for 10 to 12 hours using the BBQ sauce and spices of your choice).

🏈 Once the brisket is cooked, shred with a fork.

For the nachos

🏈 On a sheet pan (or oven safe tray) lay out the tortilla chips. Over the chips add (spread out) the sausage, cheese, beans, diced tomatoes, scallions, brisket and jalapenos (use as much or as little of everything as you want).

🏈 In a 350° oven heat the nachos for 10 minutes (until the cheese is melted and everything is warm). Remove from the oven and sprinkle with cilantro.

🏈 Serve with salsa and sour cream on the side.

> "*My parents have a version of these nachos they serve as a special in their restaurant. My Dad spends a lot of time smoking brisket in a hickory pit. I love this recipe because it's easy to assemble and you can add or subtract anything you want to it to make it your own.*"
>
> **–TED JOHNSON, NEW ENGLAND PATRIOTS 1995-2004**

TED NOW LIVES IN TEXAS WHERE HIS PARENTS OWN A RESTAURANT, THE ORIGINAL TEXAS RIB TICKLER (TEXASORIGINALRIBTICKLER.COM) AND IS THE HOST OF A WEEKDAY RADIO PROGRAM "THE TRIPLE THREAT" IN HOUSTON.

"*I love being able to talk about sports each and every day.*"

—@TEDDYJRADIO

CHRIS SPENDS MUCH OF HIS TIME WORKING ON BEHALF OF CAUSES HE BELIEVES IN. IN 2016, HE WAS INSTRUMENTAL IN BRINGING ATTENTION TO THE HEADSTRONG FOUNDATION, A CHARITY THAT IS DEDICATED TO FINDING A CURE FOR BLOOD CANCER. HE HAS HELPED THEM RAISE MORE THAN $10 MILLION FOR THEIR RESEARCH.

@CHRISHOGAN_15

CHRIS HOGAN'S
Make it Spicy Meatballs!

INGREDIENTS

For the meatballs

1	pound **ground chicken**
½	cup **cooked quinoa** *(we used Mediterranean blend)*
½	cup **panko breadcrumbs**
1	**egg**
½	teaspoon **garlic powder**
½	teaspoon **salt**
½	teaspoon **black pepper**
1-3	teaspoons **Sriracha sauce** *(depending on desired spiciness)*
1	teaspoon **honey**

For the sauce:

¼	cup **Sriracha sauce**
¼	cup **honey**
1	teaspoon **crushed garlic**

🏈 Preheat the oven to 375°.

🏈 Coat large baking tray with olive oil and set aside.

🏈 In small mixing bowl combine all the ingredients for the sauce, whisking well until smooth and set aside.

🏈 In large mixing bowl place all the ingredients for the meatballs and combine with your hands or a wooden spoon until thoroughly mixed.

🏈 With lightly damp hands roll the meat mixture into golf ball-sized rounds and transfer them to to the baking tray. Repeat until all meat has been rolled.

🏈 Bake for 20 to 25 minutes until cooked through and outside is slightly brown.

🏈 Pour the sauce over each meatball and garnish as desired.

MAKES **6** **SERVINGS**

> **"What I like about this dish is that it's got a lot of flavor but it's not a heavy tasting meatball. We like it really spicy but you can add as much heat as you want to this dish."**
> –CHRIS HOGAN, NEW ENGLAND PATRIOTS 2016-PRESENT

PICTURED: BILL BUCKNER'S BROILED TOMATOES AND GRUYERE ORZO

Sides

JOHNNY REMAINS ACTIVE WITH THE BOSTON BRUINS ORGANIZATION AND CURRENTLY SERVES AS THE TEAM'S AMBASSADOR. HE IS ACTIVE THROUGHOUT NEW ENGLAND WITH VARIOUS CHARITABLE CAUSES AND STILL RESIDES LOCALLY.

JOHNNY BUCYK'S
Tulia's Rice

INGREDIENTS

2   cups **rice**

1   medium **onion** *(finely chopped)*

2   cups **beef consommé**

1   cup **butter** *(cubed)*

1   8 ounce can **mushrooms**

1   cup chopped **mushrooms**
     (if desired)

🏒 Preheat the oven to 350°.

🏒 In a medium baking casserole combine the rice, onion, consommé and canned mushrooms.

🏒 Place the cubed butter evenly over the top of the dish.

🏒 Cover tightly with tin foil and bake for one hour.

🏒 Optional: After 40 minutes sprinkle fresh chopped mushrooms over the top and place back in the oven for the remaining 20 minutes.

MAKES 4 SERVINGS

> **"I have fond memories of this recipe because I grew up with Tulia and I'm still close with her family. She would make this all the time and it's very special to me."**
>
> **–JOHNNY BUCYK, BOSTON BRUINS 1957-1978**
> **HALL OF FAME 1981**

IN 2001 MATT AND WIFE SUSIE STARTED THE LIGHT FOUNDATION WHICH IS DEDICATED TO INSTILLING THE VALUES OF RESPONSIBILITY, ACCOUNTABILITY AND HARD WORK TO TODAY'S YOUTH THROUGH THEIR PARTICIPATION IN UNIQUE OUTDOOR LEARNING EXPERIENCES.

"I thoroughly enjoy working closely with these young people and assisting them in reaching their highest potential. Helping them become responsible members of their communities is extremely rewarding."

—MATT
@LIGHTFOUNDATION
@SUZILIGHT72
MATTLIGHT72.COM

MATT LIGHT
Susie's Pasta with Kale, Lemon and Garlic

INGREDIENTS

1 box of **pasta**
   (your choice, we used spaghetti)

3 cups **kale**
   (remove stems and finely chop)

2 tablespoons **olive oil**

2 **lemons**

2-3 *cloves of* **garlic** *(finely chopped)*

¼ cup **pine nuts**

1 teaspoon **red pepper flakes**

½ cup shredded **parmesan cheese**

   Salt

   Pepper

MAKES **6** **SERVINGS**

🏈 Cook the pasta according to the box directions.

🏈 In a large skillet, heat 1 tablespoon of olive oil, add the pine nuts, garlic, kale and red pepper flakes.

🏈 Season with salt and pepper (to taste) and sauté over medium heat until the kale is cooked (about 5 to 7 minutes).

🏈 Once the kale is cooked, add the cooked pasta, the remaining olive oil and the juice of 1 lemon.

🏈 Sprinkle with parmesan cheese, garnish with lemon and serve.

> "*Cooking in our house is somewhat challenging because my wife Susie is a vegetarian and the rest of us eat meat. So, we have a lot of recipes that can either be made using vegetables or meat. This pasta is something the whole family likes and can be a main course or side dish.*"
>
> **—MATT LIGHT**
> **NEW ENGLAND PATRIOTS 2001-2011**

"*Your kitchen will be filled with the wonderful aroma of this dish.*"

—DINAH BIRD

LARRY BIRD'S
Potato and Gruyère Gratin

INGREDIENTS

1   cup **yellow onion** (diced)

1½   tablespoons **olive oil**

2   tablespoons **unsalted butter**

2½   pounds **russet potatoes**
(peeled and sliced into ⅛" pieces)

2   medium **fennel bulbs**
(thinly sliced)

2½   cups **heavy cream**

2⅔   cups grated **Gruyère cheese**

1   teaspoon **salt**

1   teaspoon **pepper**

1   tablespoon **sage**

3   cloves **garlic** (minced)

⅓   cup **parsley** (chopped)

MAKES 8-10 SERVINGS

✱ Preheat the oven to 350°.

✱ Butter a four quart baking dish and set aside.

✱ Sautee the onions, fennel, garlic and butter over medium heat for 10 to 12 minutes until onions are translucent.

✱ In a bowl mix the sliced potatoes, 2 cups of the heavy cream, 2 cups Gruyère, sage, salt and pepper and mix the ingredients together. Slowly mix in the onion, fennel and garlic mixture until completely combined. (Be careful not to break the potatoes).

✱ Pour the mixture into the baking dish and slowly press down evenly throughout the dish (lightly press). Mix the rest of the cream and cheese together and pour over the top.

✱ Bake for 1 hour and 45 minutes.

✱ Let stand for 10 minutes and sprinkle the parsley over the top.

> **"My family and I enjoy this dish on our birthdays and on holidays."**
> **–LARRY BIRD, BOSTON CELTICS, 1979-1992**
> **BASKETBALL HALL OF FAME 1998**

FRED SMERLAS & STEVE DEOSSIE'S
Creamed Corn

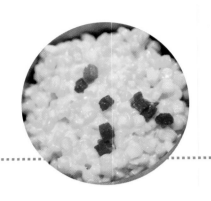

INGREDIENTS

4   ears **corn on the cob**

½   ounce **pancetta**

¼   teaspoon **granulated sugar**

½   cup **heavy cream**

MAKES **2-3** SERVINGS

🏈 Cut the corn off the cob with a knife (be careful).

🏈 In a mixing bowl place the corn, pancetta, sugar and cream and combine together until the corn is coated.

🏈 Add the mixture to a skillet over medium-high heat.

🏈 Cook everything together until the corn softens (about 5 minutes).

🏈 Serve immediately with the main course of your choice.

> "Growing up in a Greek household we had so many fantastic dishes and recipes. I still have so many fond memories of us all around the table. It gave me an appreciation of food and different flavors. What I like about this dish is that it is extremely flavorful but simple to make, which is really the best of all worlds."

**—FRED SMERLAS, NEW ENGLAND PATRIOTS 1991-1992, BOSTON COLLEGE 1976-1979
HOMETOWN: WALTHAM, MA**

"Fred grew up with Greek culinary influences and I grew up with German cooking but we both have a love of food and are committed to sharing that at our restaurant Fred & Steve's Steakhouse (Lincoln, RI). I think there's something special about being able to sit down to an incredible meal, enjoy a great glass of wine and share a dessert with family and friends."

—STEVE DEOSSIE
@STEVEDEOSSIE
@FREDANDSTEVES

MATTHEW IS EXTREMELY GENEROUS WITH HIS TIME AND IS INVOLVED IN MANY CHARITABLE EFFORTS BOTH LOCALLY AND NATIONALLY. IN 2017, HE RECEIVED THE BART STARR AWARD WHICH IS VOTED ON BY HIS NFL PEERS AND GIVEN EACH YEAR TO THE PLAYER WHO PERSONIFIES LEADERSHIP AND CHARACTER BOTH ON AND OFF THE FIELD.

MATTHEW SLATER'S
Organic Sweet Potato Casserole

INGREDIENTS

Casserole

6   large **organic sweet potatoes**

3   fresh **organic eggs**

1½ cups **organic granulated sugar**

½   teaspoon **salt**

1   tablespoon **organic vanilla extract**

1   teaspoon **organic cinnamon**

½   teaspoon **organic nutmeg** (grated)

½   cup fresh **organic butter** (melted)

Topping

1   cup organic brown sugar

¼   cup **organic flour**

½   cup **organic butter** (melted)

1   cup **walnuts** (substitute pecans, almonds, macadamia or a combination if desired)

MAKES  6-8 SERVINGS

> **"This is my favorite side dish to eat during Thanksgiving and Christmas when I take a break from my relatively clean diet and indulge! This decadent and hearty preparation of sweet potatoes satisfies even the strongest sweet tooth."**
>
> **–MATTHEW SLATER**
> **NEW ENGLAND PATRIOTS 2008-PRESENT**

🏈 Preheat the oven to 350°.

🏈 Butter a medium-size casserole dish.

🏈 Clean the sweet potatoes thoroughly and pierce them with a fork (to speed up the cooking). In a large pot, cook sweet potatoes in boiling water for 10 to 15 minutes or until soft enough to mash (do not overcook). Allow the sweet potatoes to cool (about 5 minutes).

🏈 While the potatoes are still warm, gently peel away the skin. (It should fall away from the flesh easily). In a large bowl, mash the sweet potatoes with the melted butter.

🏈 In a medium bowl beat the eggs until they are fluffy. Add the sugar, salt, vanilla, cinnamon and nutmeg and mix together until combined.

🏈 Add the egg mixture to the sweet potatoes and beat thoroughly with a mixer on a low speed until fully combined and then on medium speed until fluffy. Pour the mixture into the buttered casserole dish.

🏈 Bake for 30 to 45 minutes (depending on the depth of your pan) until the casserole is cooked through and slightly firm.

🏈 For the topping: Stir the flour, sugar and melted butter together. Slowly add the nuts until fully combined. Sprinkle the topping over the cooked casserole and bake for an additional 10 minutes.

🏈 Allow to set for 5 to 10 minutes and enjoy!

🏈 Note: For a healthier casserole, use only ½ cup of the granulated sugar, omit the butter and substitute a ¼ cup of almond, soy or coconut milk. You can also prepare the pan with a nonstick cooking spray.

RAY AND WIFE SHANNON HAVE BEEN BUSY OPENING RESTAURANTS THAT ARE 100% ORGANIC FAST FOOD CALLED GROWN™. THE GOAL IS TO MAKE HEALTHFUL, ORGANIC AND NATURAL FOODS ACCESSIBLE TO EVERYONE QUICKLY.

"I think people are getting much more conscious about what they are putting into their bodies."

—RAY @GROWNORGANICS, GROWN.ORG

RAY ALLEN'S

Shannon and Ray's grown™ Mediterranean Quinoa Tabblouleh Salad

INGREDIENTS

2	cups	**organic quinoa**
4	cups	**water**
½	tablespoon	**kosher salt**
½	cup organic	**olive oil**
½	tablespoon	**sea salt**
¼	teaspoon	**black pepper**
¼	cup fresh	**organic lemon juice**
	Zest of 1	**organic lemon**
2	cups	**organic Roma tomatoes** (diced)
1⅓	cups	**organic scallions** (diced)
1⅓	cups fresh	**organic parsley** (chopped)

✜ In a sauce pan, bring the water to a boil. Add quinoa and kosher salt and reduce heat to low, cover and simmer for 15 minutes.

✜ Remove from heat and lay out on sheet pan to cool.

✜ In a large bowl add the tomatoes, lemon zest, scallions, olive oil, sea salt, black pepper, lemon juice and parsley and stir together.

✜ Once cooled, add the quinoa to the bowl and fold all the ingredients together.

MAKES 6-8 SERVINGS

"At grown™ we are focused on organic and healthy ingredients that are locally sourced. This is our Mediterranean Quinoa Tabblouleh Salad which we serve as a side with our meals. It's both nutritious and satisfying."

–RAY ALLEN
BOSTON CELTICS 2007-2012, CONNECTICUT COLLEGE 1993-1996

BILL IS A POPULAR SPEAKER SOUGHT AFTER BY MANY COMPANIES
AND ORGANIZATIONS. HE IS CONSTANTLY TRAVELING THE COUNTRY
PARTICIPATING IN PERSONAL APPEARANCES, MEDIA, CORPORATE
EVENTS AND NUMEROUS CHARITIES.

"I like to focus on the importance of teamwork."

—BILL
(BILLBUCKNER.NET)

BILL BUCKNER'S
Broiled Tomatoes and Gruyere Orzo

INGREDIENTS

12	mini **Campari tomatoes**
2	tablespoons **olive oil**
1	cup fresh **basil** (chopped)
2½	cups **orzo**
1	cup **Gruyere cheese** (grated)
½	cup **heavy cream**
½	stick Kerrygold salted **butter**
2	teaspoons **red pepper flakes**
	Salt
	Pepper

MAKES **3-4** SERVINGS

For the orzo

☺ Prepare the orzo using the box directions (make it al dente, firm to the tooth) drain and put in a bowl.

☺ Add the butter, cream, gruyere, red pepper flakes, salt and pepper (to taste) and gently toss together with the hot orzo (do not heat this on the stove).

For the tomatoes

☺ Preheat oven to high broil.

☺ In a baking dish (or pie plate) halve the tomatoes and place them cut side up.

☺ Drizzle with olive oil (be generous). Sprinkle with basil, salt and pepper (to taste).

☺ Broil until gently charred (about 7 minutes).

> "We try and eat pretty healthy and make an effort to stick to healthier fats. These recipes are great together or individually and will work with any main course."
>
> —BILL BUCKNER,
> BOSTON RED SOX 1984-1987

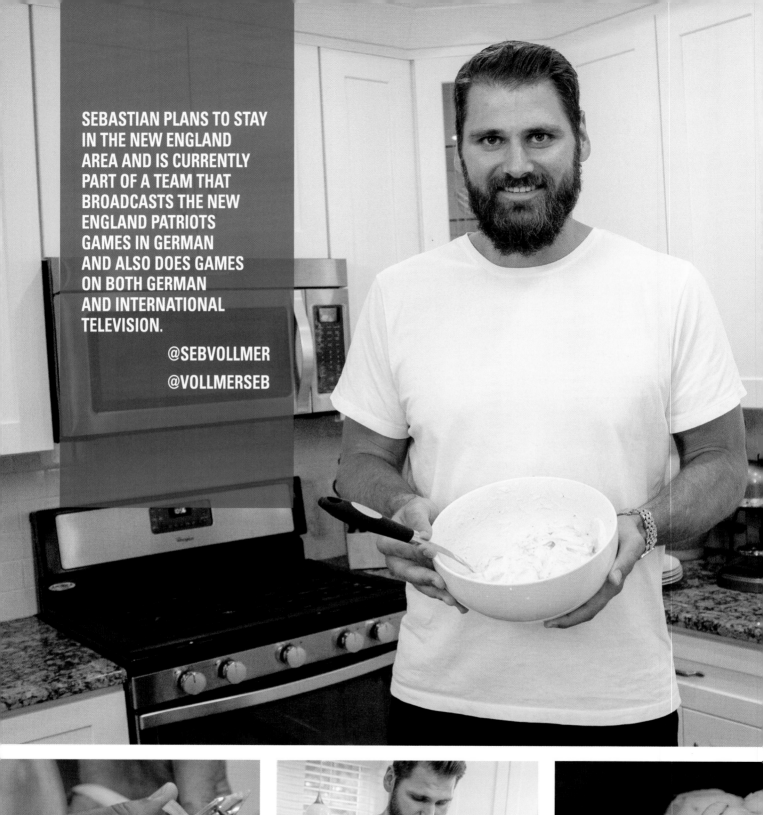

SEBASTIAN PLANS TO STAY IN THE NEW ENGLAND AREA AND IS CURRENTLY PART OF A TEAM THAT BROADCASTS THE NEW ENGLAND PATRIOTS GAMES IN GERMAN AND ALSO DOES GAMES ON BOTH GERMAN AND INTERNATIONAL TELEVISION.

@SEBVOLLMER

@VOLLMERSEB

SEBASTIAN VOLLMER'S
Düsseldorf Style Potato Salad

INGREDIENTS

6	large **red bliss** or **new potatoes** (it is very important that the potatoes be a waxy variety)
½	large **cucumber**
1	medium **onion** chopped
1½	cups of **mayonnaise**
1	cup plain **Greek yogurt**
½	cup **sour cream**
½	cup **whipping cream**
1	tablespoon **garlic powder**
1	tablespoon **black pepper**
2	teaspoons **salt**

MAKES (6-8) SERVINGS

> "I actually don't eat dairy very much at all but this recipe is my Mom's and reminds me of home. It's a good recipe for a cookout with a steak or something like that. I'm far away from my hometown of Düsseldorf, Germany and it's nice to enjoy a taste of home once in a while."
>
> **–SEBASTIAN VOLLMER, NEW ENGLAND PATRIOTS 2009-2017**

- Place the potatoes in a pot of cold water and bring to a boil over high heat. (It's important to start with the water cold).

- Boil the potatoes for 20 minutes.

- Drain and let them cool on the stove for two hours. (Do not put them into the refrigerator to cool, leave them on the stove).

- Once cool, peel the potatoes and slice them into $1/8$ inch slices and place them into a large bowl.

- In a bowl add the mayonnaise, yogurt, sour cream, whipping cream, black pepper, salt and garlic powder and stir until combined.

- Using a potato peeler, take the skin off the cucumber. Slice the cucumber very, very thin with the peeler. Add the cucumber and onion to the bowl with mayonnaise mixture and stir until combined.

- Slowly add the mixture to the bowl with the potatoes, stir it in carefully so as to not break the potatoes. Keep adding until you get the desired consistency you are looking for. Use more of the mayonnaise mixture for a wetter potato salad and less for a drier potato salad.

- This can be served at room temperature or place in refrigerator to chill the potato salad.

"*Our friends and family have enjoyed this dish from childhood to adulthood. It has been a joy to see our mothers dish become the favorite of her grandkids. We have all had the duty of crumbling corn bread muffins for Nana and it is a task that we all cherish and miss doing with her now. We hope you enjoy and love it as much as we do.*"

—DEE

DEE BROWN
Nana's Cornbread Stuffing

INGREDIENTS

1   large **egg**

2-3 **celery stalks**

1   medium **yellow onion**

2   sticks **salted butter**

6   **corn muffins**
     (we used Dunkin Donuts)

¼   cup **whole milk**

     Salt

     Pepper

MAKES **6-8** SERVINGS

✹ Preheat the oven to 350°.

✹ Dice the celery and onion, (you may cut back on the amount of onion if preferred). Melt the butter in separate skillet or pan.

✹ Once butter has melted add the celery and onion. Sauté on low heat until soft texture (about 3 to 5 minutes).

✹ In a mixing bowl physically hand crush the corn muffins. Once the celery and onions are done pour them directly over the muffins in the mixing bowl and mix together. Slowly add the milk to get your desired consistency.

✹ Beat 1 large egg and add to the mixture, mix all ingredients together well. Add salt and pepper to taste.

✹ Top the stuffing with a little butter (this will give you a nice golden crust on top). Place the mixture into the loaf baking pan, place into the pre-heated oven for 45 minutes uncovered.

✹ (Note: This stuffing can also go inside a turkey when baking).

> "**Nana's Cornbread Stuffing has always been our all-time favorite. What started out as the special dish of dressing for Thanksgiving soon became a family comfort food all throughout the year.**"
>
> **–DEE BROWN, BOSTON CELTICS, 1990-1998**

TROY BROWN'S
Mouthwatering Mac and Cheese

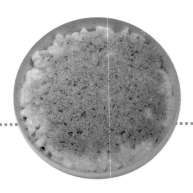

INGREDIENTS

1½ cups **elbow macaroni**
(or wheat macaroni)

1½ tablespoons **butter**

1½ tablespoons **all-purpose flour**

½ cup **yellow onion** (chopped)

½ teaspoon **minced garlic**

1 teaspoon **pepper**

1¼ cups shredded **cheddar cheese**

1¾ cups **milk**

¼ cup of **bread crumbs**

1 **tomato** (sliced)

MAKES 4 **SERVINGS**

🏈 Preheat the oven to 350°.

🏈 In two quarts of water boil the pasta with a dash of salt for 10 minutes and then drain and set aside.

🏈 While pasta is cooking, mix the butter, onions and garlic in saucepan over medium-high heat. When onions are softened (about 5 minutes) add the flour. Blend well together and then slowly add the milk. Stir until the mixture is smooth.

🏈 Add the cheese and pepper into the mixture. Make sure the cheese is completely melted into the mixture before moving on to the next step.

🏈 Once the cheese is fully combined, add the cooked elbow pasta. Pour into a two-quart casserole pan.

🏈 Sprinkle the desired amount of bread crumbs over the top.

🏈 Bake for 30 to 40 minutes.

🏈 Garnish with tomatoes (if desired).

> **"This Mac and Cheese is really creamy and flavorful and it's cheesier than most recipes. That's why I like it."**
>
> **–TROY BROWN, NEW ENGLAND PATRIOTS, 1993-2007**

"Even though I spent my entire NFL career in New England, I grew up in the South so I love Southern comfort food like this mac and cheese, steak, chicken, green beans, and collard greens. Luckily, I was able to enjoy a lot of fresh fruit, because we had it growing right in our backyard! I would pick plums, wild pears, and peaches right off the trees."

—TROY @REALTROYBROWN80

CEDRIC LEARNED HOW TO COOK AND CREATE RECIPES WITH SOME HELP FROM HIS MOTHER, WHO INSTILLED IN HIM A LOVE OF DIFFERENT CULTURES AND CUISINES.

"*What I've learned over the years with my culinary skills is that there's no easy way to perfect a recipe. It's mostly trial and error until you get it right.*"

—CEDRIC

CEDRIC MAXWELL'S
Mashed Potatoes with Gouda

INGREDIENTS

6   *baked* **potatoes**

1   *teaspoon* **black salt**

1   *stick* **butter** *(softened)*

2   *teaspoons* **Jamaican jerk seasoning**

¾   *cup* **sour cream**

½   *cup* **whole milk**

½   *teaspoon* **white truffle oil**

1   *cup* **Gouda cheese** *(shredded)*

   Himalayan sea salt

   Pepper

MAKES 6-8 SERVINGS

✺ Preheat the oven to 350°.

✺ Pierce the potatoes with a fork, sprinkle them with black salt and bake them for 60 to 75 minutes (until soft).

✺ Let them cool for 5 to 10 minutes and then scoop all the insides of the potatoes out into a pot.

✺ Add the milk, jerk seasoning, sour cream and truffle oil and mash until relatively smooth.

✺ In a pot over medium heat, add the butter and Gouda cheese and mash until it reaches your desired consistency (about 5 to 6 minutes).

✺ Salt and pepper to taste.

✺ Let sit for 3 to 5 minutes and serve.

> "The Gouda in this recipe really gives it a nice smoky flavor and taste. I like the fact that you can use these mashed potatoes with most any main course. It's extremely versatile."
>
> —CEDRIC MAXWELL
> BOSTON CELTICS 1977-1985

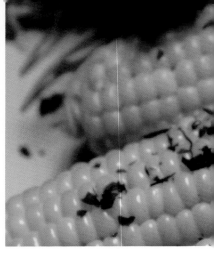

WALTER IS STILL WITH
THE BOSTON CELTICS
ORGANIZATION AS AN
ASSISTANT COACH.

"*I love getting the
opportunity to stay
involved with the
game, coach young
talent and see them
progress.*"

—WALTER
@WALTERMCCARTY

WALTER MCCARTY'S
Corn on the Cob

INGREDIENTS

5-6 *ears* **corn on the cob**

1   *lemon*

1   *tablespoon of* **sugar**

1   *tablespoon* **parsley**
    (chopped for garnish)

MAKES **5-6** SERVINGS

⚙ In a large pot of water, squeeze the juice from the lemon and pour in the sugar.

⚙ Bring the water to a boil over a high heat.

⚙ Turn the heat off and put the corn in the water.

⚙ Cover with the lid and let the corn sit in the water for 15 minutes.

⚙ Drain, sprinkle with the parsley and serve.

> "I'm from Indiana, where we pair pretty much anything and everything with corn on the cob. This is a very easy recipe and a delicious way to steam it."
> —WALTER MCCARTY
> BOSTON CELTICS 1997-2005

AYLA BROWN'S
Brussels Sprouts with Pink Himalayan Sea Salt

INGREDIENTS

20   Brussels sprouts

2   tablespoons of **coconut oil**

½   teaspoon of fine pink **Himalayan sea salt**

1   tablespoon **honey**

MAKES 4 **SERVINGS**

✽ Cut the Brussels sprouts the long way into quarters.

✽ In a sauté pan heat the coconut oil over medium-high heat and add the Brussels sprouts.

✽ Sauté the Brussels sprouts until cooked (they should start to have a char on them), sprinkle with the Himalayan sea salt and drizzle with the honey. Cook for an additional 2 minutes.

✽ Remove from the heat and transfer to a tray or bowl and serve.

"*I never really had Brussels sprouts until about two years ago at a restaurant I went to. Now, I make them all the time and absolutely love them. The coconut oil and pink Himalayan sea salt make this recipe more nutritious as I try and eat as healthy as possible.*"

–AYLA BROWN, NCAA BASKETBALL PLAYER, BOSTON COLLEGE
HOMETOWN: WRENTHAM, MA

AYLA NOW SPENDS HER DAYS WORKING ON HER MUSIC AND IS VERY INVOLVED WITH PHILANTHROPY

"I really went back and sort of started from scratch with my music. I've spent so much time over the past few years learning about every aspect of the business and I've been dedicated to writing lyrics. I really have a passion for it."

—AYLA   WWW.AYLABROWN.COM

FERDI TAYGAN'S
Turkish Green Beans with Garlic Yogurt

INGREDIENTS

For the green beans

2	pounds **green beans** (cut/broken into 2-inch pieces)
1	large while **onion** (cut lengthwise and sliced into thin semi-circles)
⅔	cup mild **olive oil**
1	cup **water**
1	can (7 ounces) whole **tomatoes** (cut into small pieces, reserve the juice)
1½	tablespoons **sugar**
1	teaspoon **kosher salt**

For the yogurt

2	cups plain **whole milk yogurt**
1	clove **garlic** (finely chopped)
½	teaspoon **kosher salt**

MAKES 6-8 SERVINGS

🎾 In a medium saucepan, sauté the olive oil and onion over medium heat until translucent (about 3 to 4 minutes).

🎾 Add the tomatoes, juice, sugar and water and bring to a boil.

🎾 Add the green beans and stir. Press the beans down into the pan and distribute evenly.

🎾 Cover and cook on a low simmer stirring occasionally. Add more water as needed to maintain a good portion of the sauce.

🎾 Cook until very tender and almost falling apart, about an hour.

🎾 Serve at room temperature with the garlic yogurt and crusty French bread.

🎾 For the yogurt: In a small bowl mix yogurt, garlic and salt together (refrigerate if necessary).

> **"My mother used to make this Turkish green bean recipe for me when I was growing up and she passed it on to my wife. It's one of my favorite dishes."**
>
> **—FERDI TAYGAN, TENNIS PLAYER**
> **HOMETOWN: FRAMINGHAM, MA**

PICTURED: DAVID ORTIZ, BIG PAPI'S PAELLA

Main Courses

JOHN HAVLICEK'S
Cape Cod Inspired Fettuccini Alfredo

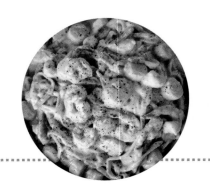

INGREDIENTS

1½   sticks of **butter** (cubed)

1½   cups of **heavy cream** or **whipping cream**

¼   cup grated **Romano cheese**

½   cup grated **Parmesan cheese**

1   pound **fettuccine noodles** (or noodles of your choice)

¾   pound **bay scallops**

¾   pound large **shrimp**

1   tablespoon **olive oil**

1   tablespoon **ground pepper**

MAKES 6 SERVINGS

✷ In a medium pot cook the noodles to your desired consistency in 2 quarts of boiling water. Drain the noodles and return the noodles to the pot.

✷ Heat the olive oil in a small skillet over medium heat. Once the oil is hot, add the shrimp and scallops and sauté until almost fully cooked (about 4 to 5 minutes). Add to the pot with the noodles and set aside.

✷ In a saucepan bring the butter and heavy cream to boil, stirring constantly.

✷ Add the cheeses by slowly sprinkling them into the mixture, stirring constantly, until the cheeses are incorporated and the mixture appears glossy (about 3 to 4 minutes). Add the pepper into the mixture.

✷ Add the sauce to the pot with the noodles and seafood over a low heat. Slowly stir until the sauce, noodles and seafood are combined. Serve immediately.

"This recipe is inspired from a restaurant I visited years ago in Lake Tahoe. We added the seafood for a little bit of a Cape Cod twist. It's something we enjoy when we want something special."

–JOHN HAVELCHIK, BOSTON CELTICS 1962-1978, HALL OF FAME 1997

JARVIS GREEN'S
Louisina Style BBQ Shrimp

INGREDIENTS

4½ pounds **Louisiana shrimp** (16/20 count), peeled and deveined with tail on)

1½ teaspoon **kosher salt**

1½ teaspoons coarsely ground **black pepper**

3 teaspoons **Creole seasoning**

1 tablespoon **thyme**

1 teaspoon minced **garlic**

⅓ cup **grapeseed oil**

½ cup dry **white wine**

2 tablespoons fresh **lemon juice**

2 tablespoons **Tabasco sauce**

1 tablespoon **Worcestershire sauce**

⅓ cup **unsalted butter** (cubed)

⅓ cup **yellow onions** (chopped)

1 teaspoon **sugar**

⅓ cup chopped **parsley** (for garnish)

2 sliced **lemons** (for garnish)

MAKES 6-8 SERVINGS

🏈 In a large bowl, combine the salt and black pepper, Creole seasoning and minced garlic.

🏈 Add the shrimp and toss well until completely coated with seasoning.

🏈 Heat a large sauté pan over medium-high heat (about 2 to 3 minutes). Add the grapeseed oil and shrimp and sauté for 1 minute. Turn the shrimp and cook for another minute.

🏈 Add white wine, lemon juice Tabasco sauce, sugar and Worcestershire sauce and cook for 1 to 2 minutes .

🏈 Add butter to the pan and swirl until melted. Add chives and thyme and remove from heat.

🏈 Garnish with parsley (and sliced lemons if desired) and serve.

> **"When I grew up we would eat dishes like this over toasted bread but now I like this dish over cornbread. This recipe has both the sweet and savory tastes that I enjoy."**
> **—JARVIS GREEN, NEW ENGLAND PATRIOTS, 2002-2009**

JARVIS NOW OWNS A SHRIMP COMPANY CALLED OCEANS 97 AND WORKS HARD TO BRING SOME SOUTHERN GOODNESS TO NEW ENGLAND.

"In the beginning I worked for free and learned the shrimping business from the ground up. When I retired we started to bring the shrimp to local retailers. Now, we are starting to bring the shrimp and our sauces to consumers. I love supporting local fishermen and families in Louisiana and sharing my recipes with others."

–JARVIS
@JARVISGREEN97

TOREY KRUG'S
Stir Fry Beef with Cauliflower Rice

INGREDIENTS

For the stir fry beef

1   pound **flank steak** *(thinly sliced)*

3   tablespoons **sugar**
     (you can substitute with
     2 tablespoons honey)

¼   cup **soy sauce**
     (you can substitute 3 tablespoons
     Coconut Aminos)

2   tablespoons **sesame oil**

1   medium **white onion** *(thinly sliced)*

2   cloves **fresh garlic** *(smashed)*

1   teaspoon **salt**

1   teaspoon **pepper**

For the rice

1   package frozen **cauliflower rice**

1   tablespoon **Coconut Aminos**

1   teaspoon **salt**

1   teaspoon **black pepper**

MAKES ④ SERVINGS

🏒 Place the steak in a mixing bowl. Add the sugar, 1 tablespoon sesame oil, soy sauce, garlic, salt and pepper. Mix well and marinate for 20 minutes.

🏒 Place 1 tablespoon of sesame oil into a frying pan over high heat for 2 minutes. Add the steak mixture and stir until brown (about 2 to 3 minutes).

🏒 Add chopped onions and reduce the heat to medium. Cover and simmer for 10 minutes.

🏒 For the cauliflower rice: In a skillet, cook the rice and heat until it becomes your desired consistency (about 3 to 4 minutes) add the Coconut Aminos, salt and pepper.

🏒 Place the rice on a platter and cover with the stir fry mixture and serve.

> **"What I like about this recipe is that it's fairly healthy and it's quick. During the season I can pretty much eat what I want but in the off-season I really make an effort to eat as healthy as possible. This is one of those dishes that is satisfying and nutritious."**
>
> **–TOREY KRUG, BOSTON BRUINS 2012-PRESENT**

IN ADDITION TO BEING AN INTEGRAL PART OF THE BOSTON BRUINS, TOREY HAS RECENTLY COMPLETED A DEGREE IN POLITICAL SCIENCE FROM MICHIGAN STATE UNIVERSITY. HE IS EXTREMELY ACTIVE IN THE COMMUNITY AND PARTICIPATES IN AS MANY CHARITABLE EFFORTS AS POSSIBLE.

"When you are as fortunate as we are, it's important to try and give back as much as possible."

—TOREY
@TOREYKRUG

MANNY RAMIREZ
My Mommy's Delicious Pork Chops

INGREDIENTS

6	**pork chops** *(regular sized, we used bone-in)*
2	**limes**
2	tablespoons **light brown sugar** *(do not substitute white or dark brown sugar)*
½	teaspoon **cumin**
1	tablespoon **oregano**
1	tablespoon **garlic powder**
1	teaspoon **salt**
½	teaspoon **black pepper**
2-3	tablespoons **olive oil**
½	cup of **vinegar**

MAKES 6 SERVINGS

> **"This recipe my Mother would make it for me since I was little and it is my absolute favorite! After every game she would have this meal prepared with love. The funny thing is that my Mom can't just cook only for one person. So my house was always full of my friends that kept coming to have her famous pork chops or I would take all the food the next day to the guys at the stadium."**
>
> **–MANNY RAMIREZ, BOSTON RED SOX 2001-2008**

☺ In a bowl combine the vinegar and two tablespoons of water.

☺ Place the pork chops on a tray and pour the vinegar and water mixture over the chops, turn them over to get both sides wet and let them soak for 2 minutes.

☺ While the pork chops are soaking, prepare the marinade. In a small bowl add the light brown sugar, cumin, oregano, salt, garlic powder and black pepper.

☺ Squeeze the juices from the limes into the mixture. Stir well until all the seasonings are combined and set aside.

☺ Rinse the pork chops at least twice with fresh water to wash out all the vinegar. Once the chops are nice and clean, put them on a baking sheet and dry them with paper towel.

☺ When the chops are dry, brush (or rub) both sides with the marinade and set aside for at least 20 minutes (you can place this in the refrigerator and marinate this for up to a day).

☺ To prepare the pork chops, take a large skillet and add olive oil to lightly coat the pan and sauté the chops until cooked (about 6 to 8 minutes per side, flip them every 3 to 4 minutes).

FRED SMERLAS & STEVE DEOSSIE'S
Porterhouse Steak for Two Hungry People

INGREDIENTS

48 ounces **porterhouse steak**

½ pound of **shallots** (chopped)

3 large **portabella mushrooms** (sliced)

1 pint of **Chianti wine**

Salt

Pepper

MAKES **2-3** SERVINGS

🏈 Let the steak sit at room temperature for 20 minutes before cooking (Note: This will help it cook quickly and more evenly). Season the steak generously with salt and pepper (to taste).

🏈 In a large skillet, pan sear the porterhouse until crust forms on each side. Due to the size of the steak it's best to transfer it to a 350° oven until the temperature reaches 125°. Slice the steak into strips.

🏈 Serve with the shallot and portabella confit.

🏈 For the shallot and portabella confit: Heat the vegetable oil in a large skillet over medium heat. Add the mushrooms and shallots then deglaze it with wine and let it reduce (about 5 to 6 minutes). Add salt and pepper (to taste).

> **"My Mother was from Germany and she had this cast iron skillet. No recipe I've had that she ever made has really tasted the same unless it was made on that skillet. I think there's just a special love passed down through that skillet with the bonding of food, friends and family over the years. I still get to enjoy it because my sister has it now, it reminds me of home"**
>
> **—STEVE DEOSSIE, NEW ENGLAND PATRIOTS 1994-1996, BOSTON COLLEGE 1980-1984**

FRED SMERLAS AND STEVE DEOSSIE HAVE OWNED FRED & STEVE'S STEAKHOUSE (LINCOLN, RI) FOR 10 YEARS.

"*What we really want to do at the restaurant is welcome people and give them a great meal. Our menu has something for everyone. We try and use freshest ingredients we can find and use them in creative ways. We want people to have the best dining experience possible.*"

—FRED SMERLAS
@FREDSMERLAS @FREDANDSTEVES

IN ADDITION TO BEING INVOLVED WITH THE BOSTON CELTICS, WALTER IS ALSO AN ACCOMPLISHED R&B SINGER.

"I've been blessed to have the opportunity to try many fun and creative things."

—WALTER

@WALTERMCCARTY

WALTER MCCARTY'S
Ginger Chicken and Sweet Potatoes

INGREDIENTS

6	boneless/skinless **chicken breasts**
8-10	small sized **sweet potatoes** (roughly cut)
1½	teaspoons **pepper**
1½	teaspoons **cumin**
2	teaspoons **salt**
5	cloves **garlic** (crushed)
3	teaspoons **ginger** (peeled and grated)
½	cup **parsley** (chopped)
4	tablespoons **olive oil**
¼	cup **honey**
1½	teaspoons **cinnamon**
1	cup chicken **broth**

MAKES  **SERVINGS**

✺ Note: This recipe can be cooked in a Dutch oven or slow cooker, if using a Dutch oven, preheat the oven to 325°.

✺ Drizzle 2 tablespoons of olive oil over the chicken breasts.

✺ Sprinkle the breasts evenly with the pepper, cumin, 3 cloves crushed garlic, 1½ teaspoons ginger, 1 ½ teaspoons salt and 1 teaspoon cinnamon.

✺ In the Dutch oven or slow cooker, add 2 tablespoons of olive oil and the sweet potatoes.

✺ Add the honey, 2 cloves crushed garlic, ½ teaspoon cinnamon, ½ teaspoon salt, 1½ teaspoons ginger, and the chicken broth.

✺ Place the chicken over the top and sprinkle with ¼ cup parsley.

✺ For the Dutch oven, cook for 2 hours. For a slow cooker, cook for 8 hours on low or 4 hours on high.

✺ Garnish with remaining parsley and serve.

> **"This recipe is great for a large group and really easy to make. It's also reasonably healthy and can be modified to taste."**
> **–WALTER MCCARTY, BOSTON CELTICS 1997-2005**

MATT LIGHT'S
Tomahawk Ribeye Steak with Chimichurri sauce

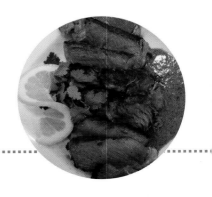

INGREDIENTS

1	32 ounce tomahawk steak (bone-in)
1	cup cilantro
1	cup flat-leaf parsley (chopped)
3	cloves garlic
3	teaspoons oregano
½	cup red onion (finely chopped)
¼	teaspoon red pepper flakes
½	cup olive oil
2	tablespoons red wine vinegar
1	lemon
	Sea Salt
	Freshly ground pepper

MAKES **4** SERVINGS

🏈 Let the steak come to room temperature, coat it with ¼ cup olive oil and season it well with salt and pepper (to taste).

🏈 Place the steak on a very, very hot grill and sear it on both sides (about 3 minutes each side).

🏈 Turn the grill down to a medium heat and continue to cook the steak for another 20 minutes (10 minutes per side). Remove from the heat and cover with foil.

🏈 For the Chimichurri sauce: In a blender, combine the cilantro, parsley, red pepper flakes, remaining olive oil, red wine vinegar and the juice of the lemon. Blend until relatively smooth. Add the onion and salt and pepper (to taste).

🏈 Once the steak has rested for 10 to 15 minutes carve and serve with a side of the Chimichurri sauce.

> **"The steak I am using is from a company called E3 Meat Company. I truly believe that they have the best meat around. I have all kinds of different meats that I keep frozen so I can use them anytime during the year. This recipe is great on its own, part of a barbeque or for special occasions. The flavor is incredible."**
>
> **—MATT LIGHT, NEW ENGLAND PATRIOTS, 2001-2011**

MATT'S ANNUAL SHOOT OUT, GAUNTLET 5K TRAIL RUN, CAMP VOHOKASE AND HIS TEAM FOR THE BOSTON MARATHON ARE JUST A FEW WAYS HE GIVES BACK THROUGH THE LIGHT FOUNDATION. HE HAS ALSO BEEN INVOLVED WITH KEEL VODKA AND IS A SOUGHT AFTER MOTIVATIONAL SPEAKER.

"I try to always be doing something, I love being part of something bigger."

—MATT
@LIGHTFOUNDATION
KEELVODKA.COM
MATTLIGHT72.COM

BRIAN SCALABRINE

Scal's Simple Salmon, Broccoli and Roasted Potatoes

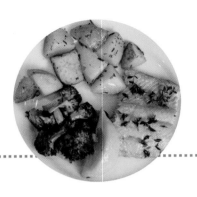

INGREDIENTS

2   pounds wild caught **king salmon filets**

6   tablespoons **olive oil**

3   **lemons** (quartered)

6   **Yukon Gold potatoes** (quartered)

2   heads **broccoli** (cut into 1 inch pieces)

½   cup fresh **thyme** (chopped

½   cup fresh **rosemary** (chopped)

     Himalayan sea salt

     Pepper

MAKES 6 SERVINGS

✳ Preheat the oven to 375°.

✳ **For the potatoes:** In a medium sized pot boil the potatoes on high for 15 minutes. Transfer to a sheet pan, coat with 2 tablespoons olive oil and sprinkle with salt, pepper, ¼ cup rosemary and ¼ cup thyme. Cook for 20 to 25 minutes until the potatoes are crispy.

✳ **For the broccoli:** On a sheet pan lay out the broccoli, coat with 2 tablespoons olive oil and sprinkle with salt and pepper (to taste). Squeeze the juice of 2 of the lemon quarters over the top. Cook for 30 minutes (turning every 10 minutes) until the broccoli is crispy.

✳ **For the salmon:** Place some tin foil over a sheet pan and place the salmon skin side down. Squeeze the juice of 4 lemons over the top. Coat with 2 tablespoons olive oil, sea salt, pepper, ¼ cup rosemary and ¼ cup thyme. Cook for 10 to 15 minutes.

✳ Plate everything and serve.

> "What we sometimes like to do with this recipe is cook the broccoli first and eat it as an appetizer. That way we make sure the kids get their vegetables and we don't need to think about that during the rest of the meal. The potatoes and broccoli can literally go with anything you want to serve."
>
> **–BRIAN SCALABRINE, BOSTON CELTICS 2005-2010**

BRIAN IS CURRENTLY A MEMBER OF THE BOSTON CELTICS BROADCAST TEAM AND IS THE CO-HOST OF "THE STARTING LINE UP" ON SIRIUSXM NBA RADIO. HE IS ACTIVE IN LOCAL CHARITY EVENTS.

"*Wild caught salmon is a staple in my house. I love grilling it in the summertime when we're just hanging out in yard.*"

—BRIAN
@SCALABRINE

JIM IS NOW THE OWNER OF GOLD MEDAL STRATEGIES. HE TRAVELS THE COUNTRY GIVING KEYNOTES.

"*I like being able help inspire and motivate companies. Great teams and quality organizations are winning ones.*"

—JIM
(WWW.GOLDMEDALSTRATEGIES.COM)

JIM CRAIG'S
Miraculous Prime Rib

INGREDIENTS

7 pound **beef prime rib** *(bone in)*

½ tablespoon **cracked black pepper**

6 **rosemary sprigs** *(3 finely chopped and 3 roughly chopped)*

½ tablespoon **fresh thyme leaves** *(chopped)*

½ tablespoon **fresh sage leaves** *(chopped)*

4 **garlic cloves** *(finely chopped)*

4 tablespoons **olive oil**

1 teaspoon **sea salt**

MAKES (8) SERVINGS

- Preheat the oven to 500°.

- Sprinkle meat with 2 teaspoons of the sea salt and let it rest on the counter for 2 to 3 hours to come to room temperature.

- In a small bowl stir together remaining sea salt, black pepper, 1 tablespoon chopped rosemary, thyme, sage, garlic cloves and the olive oil.

- Pat the roast dry with paper towels then rub all over with seasoning mix. Place into a roasting pan. Bake at 500° for 15 minutes.

- Reduce the heat to 325° and continue baking following these guidelines: 10 to 12 minutes per pound for rare, or 13 to 14 minutes per pound for medium rare and 14 to 15 minutes per pound for medium.

- Let the roast rest under foil for at least 15 minutes. Garnish with the roughly chopped rosemary sprigs and carve to desired thickness.

> **"Prime Rib is a special dish to me because my father taught me to make it so it always makes me think of him. We tend to save it for the special occasions when we are fortunate to be surrounded by family and lots of laughter and love."**
>
> **–JIM CRAIG, GOLD MEDAL OLYMPIAN 1980, BOSTON BRUINS 1980-1981**
> **HOMETOWN: NORTH EASTON, MA**

IN 1995, CAM AND HIS WIFE PAULINA FOUNDED THE THE CAM NEELY FOUNDATION FOR CANCER CARE. THEIR MISSION IS TO PROVIDE COMFORT, SUPPORT AND HOPE TO CANCER PATIENTS AND THEIR FAMILIES. TO DATE, THE FOUNDATION HAS DONATED OVER $30 MILLION TO TUFTS MEDICAL CENTER TO DESIGN, FUND AND COMPLETE PROJECTS THAT HAVE HAD A TREMENDOUS IMPACT ON THOUSANDS OF FAMILIES.

—@CAMNEELYFDN
CAMNEELYFOUNDATION.ORG

CAM NEELY
Paulina's Bolognese Sauce

INGREDIENTS

2	large **onions**, peeled
2	**carrots**, scraped
1	bulb **fresh fennel**
6	tablespoons virgin **olive oil**
24	tablespoons (3) sticks **unsalted butter**
2	teaspoons kosher **salt**
1	pound ground **pork**
1	pound ground **beef**
1	cup dry **white wine**
1	cup chopped canned tomatoes in heavy puree
1½	cups whole **milk**
½	cup chopped thyme
3	pounds **pasta** (fettucine or rigatoni)
	Small wedge **parmigiano-reggiano** (to grate for garnish, if desired)
1	teaspoon **parsley** (chopped, for garnish, if desired)

MAKES 12 SERVINGS

> **"My wife Paulina is an amazing cook. This recipe not only has excellent flavors but can feed a very, very large crowd. It's one of our favorites."**
>
> **–CAM NEELY, BOSTON BRUINS, HALL OF FAME 2005, PRESIDENT BOSTON BRUINS 2007-PRESENT**

 Finely mince the onion, carrot and fresh fennel.

 Heat the olive oil and 8 tablespoons of butter in a heavy-bottomed pot. Add the minced vegetables. Sauté over low heat, stirring occasionally, until they are very soft and have almost melted into a puree (about 30 minutes). The vegetables must be soft before proceeding with the recipe.

 Add the salt and sauté for 2 minutes. Add the meat, raise the heat and sauté. Stir until the meat is no longer pink.

 Add the wine and cook gently, (stirring occasionally), until all the wine has evaporated (about 30 minutes).

 Add the whole milk and cook on low until milk has evaporated, this may take a while. Add the tomatoes and let simmer for an additional 45 to 50 minutes on low heat (stirring often). Add thyme, stir well.

 Bring 10 quarts of salted water to a boil in a stockpot. Drop the pasta into the hot water and cook until it is still quite firm, 4 to 5 minutes.

 Drain and add the pasta to the sauce, toss for 1 to 2 minutes (until al dente). Cut up the remaining 16 tablespoons of butter and add to the pasta. Continue to toss until the butter melts and combines with the sauce.

 Top with grated cheese, parsley (if desired) and serve immediately.

CEDRIC MAXWELL'S
Surf and Turf

INGREDIENTS

For the lamb

6	lamb chops
1	cup *Robert Rothschild's Pineapple Coconut Mango Tequila Sauce*
1	cup **coconut pineapple sauce** *(we used Robert Rothschild)*
2	tablespoons **white truffle oil**
1	cup **barbeque sauce**
2	teaspoons **curry powder**
1	teaspoon **Himalayan sea salt**
1	teaspoon **pepper**
1	tablespoon **Jamaican jerk seasoning** *(we used Two Snooty Chefs)*

For the salmon

12-14	ounce **salmon filet**
2	tablespoons **basil oil**
1	tablespoon **seafood rub** *(we used Big Sur Gourmet)*
1	tablespoon **Jamaican jerk seasoning** *(we used Two Snooty Chefs)*
1	teaspoon **creole seasoning** *(we used Tony Chachere's)*

MAKES **2-3** SERVINGS

For the lamb

✹ Combine all ingredients in a mixing bowl (except the jerk seasoning) and stir until combined.

✹ Coat the lamb chops with the mixture and allow to marinate for at least 6 hours (you can also do this the day before and marinate up to 24 hours).

✹ When ready to cook, preheat the oven to 350°.

✹ Using a baking pan lined with foil, place the lamb chops (space them evenly) in the pan and sprinkle with the jerk seasoning. Cook for 35 to 40 minutes (until the lamb reaches your desired temperature).

For the salmon

✹ Preheat the oven to 350°.

✹ Place the salmon in a baking pan lined with foil. Coat the salmon with the basil oil and cover with the seafood rub.

✹ Sprinkle with the jerk seasoning, salt and pepper. Cook for 15 to 20 minutes.

✹ Let everything sit for 5 to 6 minutes and serve.

> "*What I like about this recipe is that there's sort of something for everybody here. I combined these two recipes to make a surf and turf offering, which I do a lot. The combination of the two goes well together because they share some similar seasonings. The flavors go great all together.*"
>
> **–CEDRIC MAXWELL, BOSTON CELTICS 1977-1985**

CEDRIC IS STILL INVOLVED WITH THE CELTICS AND IS PART OF THEIR RADIO BROADCASTS.

"*I love basketball and being involved with the Celtics for so many years has been a blessing. They are truly a class organization and I feel lucky to be a part of it.*"

—CEDRIC

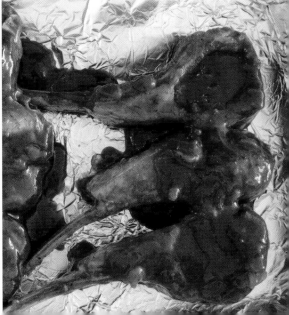

KIRK HANEFELD'S
Fancy Pants Chicken

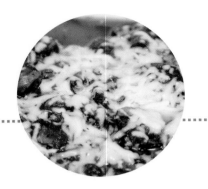

INGREDIENTS

10 chicken breasts
(very, very thinly cut)

6-8 slices **prosciutto**

1½ cups **spinach**

8 ounces **mushrooms**
(your choice, sliced)

1 envelope **Lipton Recipe Secret's Savory Herb with Garlic**

½ cup **white wine**
*(can substitute **apple cider vinegar**)*

¼ cup **olive oil**

8 ounces shredded **mozzarella cheese**

Kosher salt

Coarse Black Pepper

MAKES **5** SERVINGS

⬤ Preheat the oven to 375°.

⬤ Spray a 9x13 inch baking pan with cooking spray and add two layers of the chicken.

⬤ Cover the chicken with prosciutto, top with spinach and sprinkle with salt and black pepper. Cover the top with mushrooms.

⬤ In a bowl, whisk together olive oil, wine and savory herb and garlic envelope. Pour over the entire baking pan.

⬤ Cover loosely with foil and bake for 30 minutes.

⬤ Remove from the oven and top with the cheese.

⬤ Bake uncovered for 5 minutes and serve.

"*This recipe is a family favorite. It's great because you can make it all in one pan and the flavors go well together. It's great over rice pilaf, couscous, potatoes or pasta.*"

–KIRK HANEFELD
PGA GOLFER HOMETOWN: CLAREMONT, NH

KIRK AND WIFE KATHLEEN STILL LIVE LOCALLY. HE IS CURRENTLY A MEMBER OF THE CHAMPION'S TOUR AND THE DIRECTOR OF INSTRUCTION AT SALEM COUNTRY CLUB.

"Golf is one sport that you can enjoy no matter what your age or ability. I love helping people with the game. It's always that one great shot that keeps people coming back."

—**KIRK**
@SALEMCC1895

IN 1998, DOUG AND HIS WIFE LAURIE STARTED THE DOUG FLUTIE JR. FOUNDATION FOR AUTISM. THE FOUNDATION'S GOAL IS TO PROVIDE FAMILIES WITH A PLACE TO TURN WHEN THEY ARE IN NEED OF SUPPORT, FINANCIAL ASSISTANCE AND AUTISM RESOURCES. TO DATE, THE FLUTIES HAVE DISTRIBUTED OVER $10 MILLION FOR GRANTS AND PROGRAMS IN NORTH AMERICA.

@DOUGFLUTIE
@FLUTIEFDN
FLUTIEFOUNDATION.ORG

DOUG FLUTIE'S
New England Game Day Meatloaf

INGREDIENTS

5	pounds ground **beef** (80% lean)
1	cup **red pepper** (finely diced)
6	tablespoons **minced garlic**
½	cup **white onions** (finely diced)
¼	pound unsalted **butter**
2	ounces **milk** (2% low fat)
1	cup heavy **cream**
10	slices **white bread** (crusts removed)
5	whole **eggs**
5	tablespoons **A-1® steak sauce**
5	tablespoons **chili sauce**
3	tablespoons **beef base**
1	tablespoon **liquid smoke flavoring**
2	tablespoons **kosher salt**
1¼	tablespoons **dry oregano leaves**
1¼	tablespoons **black pepper**
2	cups plain **bread crumbs**
½	cup **parsley** (finely chopped)

MAKES 20-25 **SERVINGS**

Preheat the oven to 300°.

In a thick braising pan heat the butter over medium heat until it's melted. Add the onions, peppers and garlic. Sauté approximately 5 minutes until lightly caramelized. Set aside to cool or place in the refrigerator.

While sautéing vegetables, pour heavy cream and milk over white bread in a mixing bowl; soak up liquid. Place in food processor (or use your hands) to puree smooth (no lumps).

In a separate mixing bowl, whisk together eggs, chili sauce, A-1 sauce, beef base, salt, pepper, oregano and liquid smoke. Mix well to dissolve all the beef base. Then add the parsley and breadcrumbs.

In another large bowl, mix the meat and add all the remaining ingredients. Mix thoroughly with hands until everything is fully combined. Place mix on top of full size parchment paper.

Using the paper, mold and press back and forward. This will take all the air bubbles from the mix. Shape into a square or oblong log, 4 inch high (the ends should be flat). Place loaf on a sheet pan.

Bake the meatloaf for 1.25 hours.

> "This is a recipe we serve at my restaurant, Flutie's Sports Pub (Plainville, MA). It's great for a winter or fall New England day. If you're having people over for a game, it feeds a large crowd."
>
> –DOUG FLUTIE, NEW ENGLAND PATRIOTS 1987-1989, 2005
> BOSTON COLLEGE 1981-1984, HOMETOWN: NATICK, MA

TUUKKA RASK'S
Sweet Potato Gnocchi with Spicy Sausage and Bacon

INGREDIENTS

3	**spicy Italian sausages** *(chopped into 1" pieces)*
5	slices **bacon** *(chopped into ½" pieces)*
1	cup **asparagus** *(chopped into 1" pieces)*
½	cup **onion** *(chopped)*
3	cloves **garlic** *(chopped)*
1	**tablespoon thyme** *(chopped)*
⅓	cup **mascarpone cheese**
1	teaspoon **salt**
1	tablespoon **pepper**
⅓	cup **olive oil**
¼	cup shredded **Parmesan cheese**
1	package frozen **sweet potato gnocchi**

MAKES 3-4 SERVINGS

🏒 In a medium skillet, heat the olive oil until hot. Add garlic, onion, Spicy Italian sausage, and bacon until brown (about 5 minutes).

🏒 Add the asparagus, salt, pepper and thyme and cook over medium heat for 3 to 4 minutes.

🏒 Over high heat boil 2 quarts of water, add the sweet potato gnocchi and cook for the 2 minutes until the gnocchi starts to rise in the pot (be careful not to over-cook) and drain.

🏒 Add the mascarpone cheese to the sausage, bacon and asparagus mixture and stir until the cheese is melted, then stir in the gnocchi.

🏒 Serve while hot and sprinkle with Parmesan cheese (if desired).

> **"**Since I left home at 16 to pursue hockey, I had to learn to cook for myself or I was going to go hungry. Now I cook a lot for myself and my family. This recipe is quick, tastes great and is something I enjoy making.**"**
>
> —TUUKKA RASK, BOSTON BRUINS 2007-PRESENT

TUUKKA SPENDS A LOT OF TIME PARTICIPATING IN CHARITABLE CAUSES AND IS IN THE PROCESS OF CREATING THE TUUKKA RASK FOUNDATION.

"We [athletes] have been given so much in life, it is important to give back as much as possible. That is something that I believe in and the Boston Bruins organization is committed to as well."

—TUUKKA
@TUUKKARASK

DAVID'S FOUNDATION, THE DAVID ORTIZ CHILDREN'S FUND IS DEVOTED TO HELPING CHILDREN IN THE DOMINICAN WHO NEED HEART SURGERIES, AS WELL AS PROVIDE SUPPORT FOR FAMILIES IN NEW ENGLAND WHO HAVE A CHILD LIVING WITH CONGESTIVE HEART DISORDERS (CHD).

"Helping children anywhere is a cause close to my heart."

—DAVID
@DAVIDORTIZ

DAVIDORTIZCHILDRENSFUND.ORG

DAVID ORTIZ'S
Big Papi's Paella Recipe

INGREDIENTS

3	tablespoons **olive oil**
3	pounds **chicken wings**
2	cups **risotto** (or **arborio rice**)
1	**green pepper** (sliced)
1	**red pepper** (sliced)
1	large **yellow onion** (sliced)
4-6	cups **chicken broth**
¼	cup **white wine** (we used Arias)
1	pound cooked **shrimp**
1	½ cups frozen **peas**
1	28 ounce can **tomatoes** (drained)
1½	cups **linguica sausage** (cooked, sliced into ¼ inch pieces and halved)
1	tablespoon **Annatto seasoning**
2	teaspoons **Adobo seasoning**
	Salt
	Pepper

MAKES 8 SERVINGS

⚾ In a paella pan (or extra-large fry pan) heat the olive oil over medium-high heat. Salt and pepper the chicken wings and place them in the pan to brown (about 6 minutes). Remove the chicken wings and set aside.

⚾ Add the green pepper, red pepper and onion to the pan and sauté for 5 minutes.

⚾ Slowly add the rice, 4 cups of the both, wine, Annatto and Adobo seasonings to the mixture and let simmer for 20 minutes.

⚾ Add the chicken back into the pan and continue to simmer for 15 minutes. Continue to stir every 5 minutes and add additional broth (if needed ¼ cup at a time to have the rice reach your desired consistency).

⚾ Add the frozen peas and sausage and simmer for an additional 5 to 6 minutes.

⚾ Finally, add the cooked shrimp and stir for 3 minutes.

⚾ Remove from the heat and allow to sit 5 to 10 minutes before serving.

> **"I like traditional recipes which are full of different flavors and ingredients. Paella has so many of the spices and tastes of the Dominican. It's a great dish to share with family and friends."**
>
> –DAVID ORTIZ, BOSTON RED SOX 2003-2016

ANDRE TIPPETT
Stuffed Bone-In Veal Chop

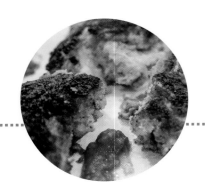

INGREDIENTS

4   10 ounce **veal chops**

4   slices **prosciutto** (thinly sliced)

6   ounces **fontina cheese** (cut into 1" rounds)

10-12   ounces **mushrooms** (mixture of any types, baby bella, shiitake, etc.)

1   **shallot** (chopped)
5   tablespoons **butter**
3   tablespoons **olive oil**
6   **garlic cloves** (crushed)
1   cup all-purpose **flour**
3   **eggs** beaten

2   cups of **panko breadcrumbs** (seasoned with 1 teaspoon each salt, pepper, and garlic powder)
    salt
    pepper

MAKES (4-6) SERVINGS

> "*The juiciness of this veal with the combination of the stuffing is so good and tasty. It is a great satisfying meal and it's not something you feel that guilty about afterwards. My wife Ronda and I usually add a side of pasta and salad with this.*"
>
> **–ANDRE TIPPETT**
> **NEW ENGLAND PATRIOTS 1982-1993**
> **HALL OF FAME 2008**

🏈 To prepare the veal, pound each chop slightly (it should be long and thin enough to fold) add salt and pepper on both sides and set aside.

🏈 In a medium size skillet, heat 1 tablespoon of olive oil and 1 tablespoon of butter. Add mushrooms, shallots and crushed garlic. Sauté the mixture on a medium to low heat for approximately 15 minutes, until soft. Remove from heat and set aside.

🏈 Lay out each piece of veal and layer it with a slice of prosciutto, some of the mushroom mixture and two slices of fontina cheese. Fold over and secure with toothpicks.

🏈 Dredge each veal chop in flour (shake off excess), then dip into the eggs and then transfer into bowl with panko breadcrumb mixture. Make sure you coat both sides heavily and evenly with the breadcrumbs. Repeat for all four of the chops.

🏈 In a large skillet, heat the remaining olive oil and butter. Place all four veal chops into the pan and cook on a medium to low heat, frequently turning as to not burn the breadcrumbs. Cooking varies, but will take approximately 15-20 minutes.

🏈 Plate the veal chops and drizzle with marinara sauce. Serve with a side of pasta (if desired).

ANDRE HAS BEEN INVOLVED WITH MARTIAL ARTS FOR OVER FOUR DECADES AND STILL LIVES IN MASSACHUSETTS. HE CURRENTLY SERVES AS THE EXECUTIVE DIRECTOR OF COMMUNITY AFFAIRS FOR THE NEW ENGLAND PATRIOTS

"I like the variety of seasons, food and culture of New England. This will always be home."

—ANDRE
@ANDRETIPPETT

ALICIA IS A TEN TIME OLYMPIC MEDALIST AND ONE OF THE MOST DECORATED OLYMPIANS OF ALL TIME. SHE IS ACTIVE IN THE COMMUNITY AND FOR ALICIA IT'S ALL ABOUT FAMILY

"My family is the most important thing in my life."

—ALICIA

ALICIA SACRAMONE-QUINN

Gnocchi with Sautéed Filet and Asparagus

INGREDIENTS

2-3 **beef tenderloin filet**s (cubed)

1 package **potato gnocchi**

1 bunch of **asparagus** (diced)

4-6 tablespoons **butter** (substitute **olive oil** if desired)

1-2 cloves of garlic (crushed)

½ **shallot**

1-2 teaspoons **tomato paste**

¼ cup **brandy**

¼ cup good **red wine**

Salt

Pepper

MAKES (4) SERVINGS

> **"I love to cook and this dish is a favorite of ours. It is a good source of protein and carbohydrates and it has a lot flavor."**
>
> **–ALICIA SACRAMONE-QUINN**
> **OLYMPIC GYMNAST**
> **HALL OF FAME 2015**
> **HOMETOWN: BOSTON, MA**

 For the demi-glace sauce: Melt 2 tablespoons of butter in a small frying pan. Add the two cloves of crushed garlic & the minced shallot and sauté for 1 to 2 minutes and set aside.

 Cut filets in small cube like pieces and sauté in a frying pan with 2 tablespoons of the butter for about 4 to 5 mins.

 Remove cooked filets and juices from the frying pan and transfer into a bowl (make sure to keep the juices in with the filets).

 In the same frying pan sauté diced up asparagus with some salt and pepper (to taste). Cook asparagus for about 5 to 7 minutes. Add cooked asparagus to the bowl with filets.

 Add 2 tablespoons of butter (or olive oil) to the same pan and sauté the uncooked gnocchi until they get a golden brown color to them.

 Return all ingredients to the frying pan and add demi-glace sauce and mix thoroughly.

 Slowly add the tomato paste and stir. Add brandy and red wine for 2 to 3 minutes to allow the alcohol to cook off and the mixture to thicken.

 Let sit for 3 to 5 minutes and serve.

CHARLIE MOORE'S
Grilled Backstrap Venison Medallions

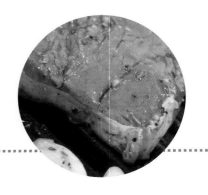

INGREDIENTS

6   *2-3 ounce backstrap venison medallions (from your local butcher)*

½   *good* **extra virgin olive oil**

2   *tablespoons* **Charlie Moore Mediterranean Spice™**

1   *teaspoon* **Charlie Moore Garlic Powder™**

4   *cloves* **garlic** *(roughly chopped)*

2   *lemons*

½   *cup* **Kikkoman soy sauce**

MAKES (3-4) SERVINGS

Place the backstrap venison medallions in a bowl and add the olive oil, soy sauce and garlic.

Add the Charlie Moore Mediterranean Spice, Charlie Moore Garlic Powder and mix until the meat is coated (this dish does not need to be marinated before-hand, it will season perfectly within minutes).

Squeeze the juice of 1 lemon into the mixture.

Over the stove, heat a grill pan over high heat for 3 to 4 minutes (do not coat the pan with olive oil or butter).

Pour the contents of the entire bowl into the grill pan and sear the medallions on each side for 3 to 5 minutes (until the center of the medallions are pink).

Squeeze the juice of 1 lemon over the top during cooking.

Serve immediately with the cooked garlic.

> **"I think when people come over it's nice to try and do something special. People always unite and have a good time over good food. It really doesn't take much to make a dining experience unique and make people happy."**
>
> **–CHARLIE MOORE, THE MAD FISHERMAN**
> **HOMETOWN: CHESTER, NH**

"It's very important to love what you do. I've been fortunate to be able to love what I do and have a great time doing it. That's why it's always been important for me to give back as much as possible."

—CHARLIE
WWW.CHARLIEMOORE.COM

REBECCA LOBO
Nana Lobo's Chicken

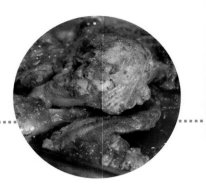

INGREDIENTS

3	pounds whole **chicken** (cut into pieces)
½	cup **onion** (chopped)
2	teaspoons **paprika**
2	teaspoons **oregano**
2	teaspoons garlic **powder**
2	teaspoons **celery salt**
1	bottle **Catalina salad dressing**
1	cup **ketchup**
3	drops **Gravy Master**

MAKES 6 SERVINGS

✹ In a large bowl, mix the paprika, oregano, garlic powder and celery salt. Rub the mixture on all the chicken pieces.

✹ Add the onion, Catalina dressing, ketchup and Gravy Master to the bowl.

✹ Slowly add the chicken one piece at a time, mix well and cover with tin foil. Allow the mixture to marinate in the refrigerator for an hour or until ready to cook.

✹ When ready to cook, remove the chicken pieces from the bowl and place in a shallow baking pan and cover with foil.

✹ Bake 2 hours at 350°. (Remove foil during last hour of baking).

✹ This dish can be served warm, room temperature or cold.

> ❝This recipe was passed to me from my paternal grandmother, Catherine Lobo, my 'Nana' to my Mom. Nana was not the best cook, but this was one recipe that was always a big hit. I loved when my mom made it and now my kids like when I make it. The new generation changed the name from 'Mama Lobo's Chicken' to 'Nana Lobo's Chicken' but the recipe has remained the same.❞
>
> –REBECCA LOBO, WNBA BASKETBALL PLAYER 1997-2003
> UNIVERSITY OF CONNECTICUT 1991-1995, HALL OF FAME 2017
> HOMETOWN: HARTFORD, CT

REBECCA IS NOT ONLY AN ANALYST FOR ESPN, SHE IS AN EXTREMELY BUSY MOM OF FOUR ACTIVE CHILDREN WHO LIKE TO HELP IN THE KITCHEN. SHE JUGGLES ALL OF IT WITH GRACE, SENSE OF HUMOR AND TRIES TO BE AS ORGANIZED AS POSSIBLE.

"As a Mom, I appreciate any recipe that is easy and can be made ahead of time."

—REBECCA
@REBECCALOBO

WHEN FRED'S NOT COOKING, HE AND WIFE NATALIE HELP SUPPORT THE ANIMAL CHARITY, FACE FOUNDATION. THE FOUNDATION PROVIDES FINANCIAL ASSISTANCE TO HELP COVER THE COST OF CRITICAL OR LIFE-SAVING VETERINARY CARE. TO DATE OVER 1,750 PETS HAVE BEEN SAVED.

—FRED
@19FREDLYNN, FREDLYNN.NET, FACEP4PETS.ORG

FRED LYNN'S
New England Style Dirty Rice

INGREDIENTS

1½	cups **wild rice** *(use a brand with a mix of texmati, brown, red, etc.)*
1½	cups diced **orange, yellow** and **red peppers**
1	pound **boneless skinless chicken breast**
1	pound **ground pork**
1	pound large **shrimp** *(uncooked)*
⅓	cup **pepperoncini** or **banana peppers** *(sliced)*
1½	cups **chicken broth** **cajun hot pepper sauce** *(to taste)* **cajun seasoning** *(to taste)*
3	tablespoons **olive oil** salt pepper

MAKES  4-6 SERVINGS

🙂 In a medium pot, prepare the rice mix using the chicken broth over medium heat (about 20 minutes).

🙂 Sautee shrimp in 1 tablespoon of oil (about 5 minutes), place in bowl and set aside.

🙂 Sautee pork and chicken in 1 table-spoon of olive until cooked (about 5 to 10 minutes), add some Cajun seasoning to mixture (to taste).

🙂 Sautee peppers and pepperoncini (or banana peppers) in 1 tablespoon olive oil until tender (about 5 minutes).

🙂 Combine all ingredients in one large pot and stir (add the Cajun hot pepper sauce, Cajun seasoning, salt and pepper to taste).

🙂 If you like it really spicy, you can serve it with a side of cottage cheese to cool the palate.

> **"*I love to cook. Since part of my ancestry is French Indian from Louisiana, I just love spicy dishes. However, my wife, Natalie, is from New England and prefers most dishes a little bit milder. So, I think of this as a compromise. You can heat it up with more of the spices or keep it cool and mild.*"**
>
> **–FRED LYNN**
> **BOSTON RED SOX 1974-1980**

SHAWN THORNTON'S
Ribeye and Brussels Sprouts

INGREDIENTS

1   *12 to 14 ounce* **ribeye**
(bone in)

½   *pound* **Brussels sprouts** *(shaved)*

3-4 *slices* **bacon**
(cut into small pieces)

¼   *teaspoon* **red pepper flakes**

Sea salt

Pepper

MAKES 1-2 SERVINGS

● Give the ribeye and the Brussels sprouts a good coating of salt and pepper (to taste).

● Once the ribeye is room temperature, cook the sirloin in a fry pan over medium-high heat for about 10 to 12 minutes (turn the ribeye after 5 to 6 minutes).

● In another fry pan, heat the olive oil over medium heat (about 2 minutes). Add the bacon and sauté until crispy (about 3 minutes). Slowly add the Brussels sprouts and sauté for 12 to 14 minutes. Sprinkle with red pepper flakes.

● When the ribeye has reached your desired temperature and the Brussels sprouts have reached your desired consistency, let sit for 5 minutes and enjoy!

> "*This recipe is very, very simple but it was what I ate every night before a game. No matter what city I was in, this was always my dinner of choice. It eliminates the carbs but it is flavorful and not overly heavy.*"
>
> **—SHAWN THORNTON**
> **BOSTON BRUINS 2007-2014**

YEARS AGO SHAWN CREATED THE SHAWN THORNTON FOUNDATION. THE CHARITY IS DEDICATED TO ASSISTING THOSE AFFECTED BY CANCER AND PARKINSON'S DISEASES. TWO CAUSES THAT ARE CLOSE TO HIS HEART. HE CURRENTLY WORKS IN THE FLORIDA PANTHERS FRONT OFFICE BUT COMES BACK TO BOSTON QUITE OFTEN.

"New England is where I feel the most comfortable, it will always be home."

- SHAWN @THORNTONFDN, THORNTONFOUNDATION.ORG

BRAD IS CURRENTLY A GOLF ANALYST FOR FOX AND EXTREMELY INVOLVED WITH PHILANTHROPIC EFFORTS. YEARS AGO, ALONG WITH FELLOW GOLFER BILLY ANDRADE, BRAD FORMED THE BILLY ANDRADE/ BRAD FAXON CHARITIES FOR CHILDREN, INC., A NON-PROFIT ORGANIZATION THAT HAS DONATED MILLIONS TO NEEDY CHILDREN.

"It's a great feeling to be able to give back."

—BRAD @BRADFAXON

BRAD FAXON'S
Pasta All'Amatriciana

INGREDIENTS

1	large **white onion** (chopped)
7	sliced **pancetta** (diced)
2	28 ounce cans whole **tomatoes** (two different types)
2	gloves **garlic** (crushed)
2	cups **Pecorino Romano cheese** (shaved)
1	teaspoon **salt**
2	teaspoons **pepper**
2	tablespoons **olive oil**
1	12 ounce box of **pasta noodles** (we used **Casarecce**)

MAKES **6** SERVINGS

🌐 Heat the olive oil in a large sauce pot (or Dutch oven) and sauté the onion and garlic until lightly brown (about 3 minutes).

🌐 Add the pancetta and garlic and continue to sauté for an additional 4 to 5 minutes.

🌐 Pour the tomatoes in a large bowl and squeeze them with your hands until no big chunks are left.

🌐 Add the tomatoes, salt and pepper to the pot and cook on low heat for an hour.

🌐 Cook the pasta using box directions and drain.

🌐 Add the pasta and 1 ½ cups of cheese to the pot and stir until all ingredients are combined.

🌐 Serve in bowls and sprinkle the top with the remaining cheese.

> **"When I played at the Masters, we rented a house and one of the guys with us would make this recipe. It's absolutely one of my favorite recipes and it became a tradition. I think using the two different brands of whole tomatoes gives the dish more flavor."**
>
> **–BRAD FAXON, PGA GOLFER**
> **HOMETOWN: BARRINGTON, RI**

PEDRO AND WIFE CAROLINA HAVE CREATED THE THE PEDRO MARTINEZ CHARITY. TO DATE, THE CHARITY HAS CHANGED OVER 400 CHILDREN'S LIVES BY USING A HOLISTIC APPROACH TO FOOD, EDUCATION, JOB TRAINING, FAMILY THERAPY AND EXTRA-CURRICULAR ACTIVITIES.

"Our mission is to give these children hope today and life skills for a future tomorrow."

—CAROLINA
@45PEDROMARTINEZ
PEDROMARTINEZCHARITY.ORG

PEDRO MARTINEZ'S
Sancocho Plate

INGREDIENTS

- 2 **lamb chops** (*boneless cut into pieces*)
- 1 **whole chicken** (*cut into pieces*)
- 4 **smoked pork chops** (*boneless cut into pieces*)
- ½ rack **pork ribs** (*cut into individual pieces*)
- 2 **yellow onions** (*sliced*)
- 3 ears **corn on the cob** (*broken into 2 to 3 inch pieces*)
- 2 teaspoons **Adobo** *seasoning*
- 2 teaspoons **Sazón** *seasoning*
- 2 cloves **garlic** (*crushed*)
- 1 pound **yucca** (*if available, peeled and cut into 1 inch pieces*)
- 1 small **butternut squash** (*peeled and cut into 2 inch pieces*)
- 4 **green bananas** (*peeled and cut into 2 pieces*)
- 2 teaspoons **orange zest**
- 2 teaspoons dried **oregano**
- 5 cups **chicken broth**
- 5 cups **water**
- ¼ cup **cilantro**
- ½ cup **celery**
- 4 tablespoons **olive oil**
- 3 **cups white rice** (*cooked, if desired*)
- 2 **avocados** (*sliced, if desired*)
- **salt**
- **pepper**

⚾ Season all the meat with Sazón seasoning, Adobo, oregano, salt and pepper (to taste).

⚾ In a large stock pot over medium heat, add the olive oil and sear chicken, lamb chops, pork chops and ribs. Add the onion, garlic and oregano and cook for 20 minutes.

⚾ Add the chicken broth, corn on the cob, yucca, squash, celery, bananas, salt and pepper (to taste) and bring to a boil over medium-high heat. Reduce the heat and simmer for 1 ½ hours. Add the orange zest and cilantro and simmer for another 30 minutes.

⚾ Serve with rice and avocado slices (if desired)

MAKES 8 SERVINGS

> **"This recipe is based on a traditional Sancocho, which is a Dominican stew made with meat and vegetables. It has a good selection of ingredients and some nice flavors that go well all together. I hope you enjoy it."**
>
> **–PEDRO MARTINEZ**
> **BOSTON RED SOX 1998-2004, HALL OF FAME 2015**

"This recipe is based on one that I used to have all the time at a restaurant in Springfield, Massachusetts. They had the best Veal Francaise I have ever had. I hope you enjoy this one."

—TOMMY HEINSOHN, BOSTON CELTICS 1956-65
BOSTON CELTICS COLOR ANALYST 1981-PRESENT

TOMMY HEINSOHN'S
Veal Francaise

INGREDIENTS

8 **veal cutlets** (boneless)

2 cups all-purpose **flour**

3 large **eggs** (beaten)

1 cup **unsalted butter** (melted)

¾ cup **heavy cream**

¾ cup **chicken broth**

¼ cup **dry white wine**

1 teaspoon **garlic salt**

1 teaspoon **pepper**

3 **lemons**

3 tablespoons **parsley** (chopped)

MAKES 8 **SERVINGS**

⚜ Lightly pound the veal and flatten into thin cutlets (about ¼ inch thick). Sprinkle the cutlets with garlic salt and pepper.

⚜ Take one cutlet, dip into the flour and then into the beaten egg mixture. Repeat for each cutlet.

⚜ In a large skillet, melt ¾ cup of the butter and brown the veal medium-high heat (3 to 4 minutes each side). Remove veal, place on a plate and set aside.

⚜ In the same skillet, add the heavy cream, chicken broth, wine, the juice of 2 lemons and stir. Bring to a boil over medium heat (stir occasionally).

⚜ Add the veal back into the skillet and add the remaining butter. Reduce the heat to low and simmer for 3 to 5 minutes (until the veal is coated and the mixture slightly thickens).

⚜ Serve the veal on a platter and cover with the sauce.

⚜ Sprinkle with the chopped parsley and garnish with lemon slices (if desired).

IN 2017, RAY TRAVELED FROM HIS HOME STATE OF TEXAS TO MASSACHUSETTS TO BE INDUCTED INTO THE NEW ENGLAND PATRIOTS HALL OF FAME.

"It's incredible to see the area and what the stadium and Patriot Place has become. It's an honor to be elected to the Patriots Hall of Fame and to have had my time here in New England."

—RAY

RAY CLAYBORN'S
Louisiana Style Gumbo

INGREDIENTS

1	whole chicken *(cut into pieces)*
1	pound **smoked garlic sausage** *(cut into ½ inch rounds)*
1	pound **raw shrimp** *(peeled and deveined)*
4	smoked **turkey necks**
1	**red pepper** *(diced)*
1	**green pepper** *(diced)*
1	**yellow pepper** *(diced)*
1	**orange pepper** *(diced)*
2	**yellow** or **green onions** *(diced)*
2	tablespoons **minced garlic**
2	tablespoons **salt**
2	tablespoons **pepper**
2	tablespoons **Tony Chachere's Creole seasoning**
2	teaspoons **garlic powder**
3	tablespoons **parsley** *(chopped)*
1	cup all-purpose **flour**
1	cup **vegetable oil**
2	tablespoons **olive oil**
5	cups **water** *(or chicken broth)*

MAKES (8) SERVINGS

> Place the chicken and the sausage in a baking pan, sprinkle with the olive oil, 1 tablespoon salt and 1 tablespoon pepper and bake at 300° for an hour.

> In a cast iron pot over medium heat, start making the roux with the flour and the vegetable oil. You will need to stir this continuously for at least 45 minutes to an hour to get a nice chocolate color to the roux. (This is the key to this gumbo, make sure it does not burn).

> Using a large pot or Dutch oven, fill it half way with the water (or the broth) and bring to a slow boil over medium heat. Add all the peppers, turkey necks, onions, garlic and stir for 4 to 5 minutes. Drop in the roux and reduce to a simmer.

> Once the roux has been incorporated, add the Creole seasoning, garlic powder, chicken, sausage and the remaining salt and pepper. Simmer for 1 ½ hours (stirring occasionally).

> Add the parsley and the shrimp and simmer for an additional 30 minutes (stirring occasionally). Add any additional seasonings of your choice (to taste).

> Serve over rice (if desired).

> **"This gumbo is one of my absolute favorites. It's great any time but when it's cold, it's even better. It just sticks to your ribs and warms you up. It takes a long time but every time my wife Kimberly and I make it, it's well worth the wait."**
>
> **–RAY CLAYBORN**
> **NEW ENGLAND PATRIOTS 1977-1989**

COLIN IS BUSY TRAVELING THE WORLD PERFORMING AND HAS A CLOTHING LINE COMING OUT SOON.

"*I absolutely love what I do and if it brings happiness to someone for even a moment I am grateful. I am so blessed to be able to have the chance to do this each and every day.*"

—COLIN
@COLINGRAFTON

COLIN GRAFTON'S
Sweet Chili Coconut Chicken

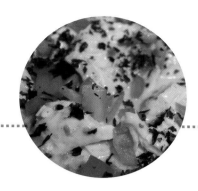

INGREDIENTS

4	medium **chicken breasts** (boneless, skinless)
3	tablespoons **olive oil**
1	teaspoon **white pepper**
1	teaspoon **salt**
1½	cans **coconut milk** (do not use low fat)
⅓	cup **sweet chili sauce**
1	medium **red pepper** (cut into small squares)
1	tablespoon **ginger** (finely chopped)
2	tablespoons fresh **parsley** (finely chopped)
2	cups **rice** (cooked, your choice)
	Parchment paper

MAKES 4 SERVINGS

> *"This recipe has been in my family for some time and we all love it. Even when I'm traveling I try and make it. The chicken is so tender it melts in your mouth."*
>
> **–COLIN GRAFTON, FIGURE SKATER
> HOMETOWN: NORTH ATTLEBORO, MA**

⛸ Preheat the oven to 400°.

⛸ Using a 9x13 inch baking pan, rub the pan and one side of the parchment paper with 1 tablespoon of the olive oil (to prevent the chicken from sticking).

⛸ Coat the chicken with the remaining olive oil and sprinkle with the salt and white pepper.

⛸ Transfer the chicken to the baking dish and lay the parchment paper over it (oil side down). Tuck in the edges of the parchment paper so that it is snug around the chicken (make sure the chicken is fully covered).

⛸ Bake the chicken for 35 to 40 minutes (temperature should be 165°).

⛸ When the chicken is cool (about 20 minutes) cut into medium-size pieces and set aside.

⛸ In a large saucepan, pour in the coconut milk and heat on a low heat until blended. Add the chopped ginger, sweet chili sauce and red pepper (save 2 tablespoons of the red pepper for garnish). Heat the mixture until bubbly.

⛸ Slowly add the cooked chicken and heat until everything is combined (about 5 to 10 minutes).

⛸ Serve with rice of your choice and garnish with the remaining red pepper and parsley (if desired).

BILLY CONIGLIARO'S
Homemade Italian Meatballs and Sausage

INGREDIENTS

Sauce:

3	tablespoons virgin **olive oil**
2	cloves **garlic**
6	**Italian spicy sausage** *(cut into pieces)*
6	ounces **salt pork**
2	12 ounce cans **peeled tomatoes**
1	12 ounce can **tomato puree**
1	12 ounce can **crushed tomatoes**
1	6 ounce can **tomato paste**
1	cup **water**
¼	cup **sugar**
5	fresh **basil leaves**
2	tablespoon **kosher salt**
½	teaspoon crushed **red pepper**
1	tablespoon **black pepper**
2	tablespoons **all-purpose seasoning**
½	teaspoon **Lawry's season salt**
2	cups **red wine**

Meatball and Sausage

3	pounds **ground beef** (75% percent lean)
2	**eggs**
⅔	cup **whole milk**
5	**basil leaves** *(finely chopped)*
1	**clove garlic** *(minced)*
4	teaspoons **Worcestershire sauce**
1	cup **Parmesan cheese** *(grated)*
1	cup **Romano cheese** *(grated)*
¼	cup flavored **Italian bread crumbs**
½	teaspoon **kosher salt**
½	teaspoon **Lawry's season salt**
½	teaspoon **black pepper**
8	**Italian sausages**

MAKES **8** SERVINGS

For the Sauce:

In a large pot over medium heat, add olive oil and garlic. Once the garlic is brown (about 3 minutes) add the whole peeled, crushed, puree tomatoes, tomato paste, fresh basil leaves, kosher salt, black pepper and all-purpose seasoning (season to taste).

Once everything is combined, add the sugar and red wine. Stir all the ingredients together, cover the pot and let it simmer for 10 to 15 minutes.

For the Meatballs:

In a large bowl, combine the ground beef, eggs, milk, basil leaves, garlic, teaspoon Worcestershire sauce, Parmesan cheese, Romano cheese, flavored Italian bread crumbs, kosher salt, black pepper and Lawry's season salt. Mix well and form into 15 to 20 balls.

Add the meatballs and sausage to the sauce and make sure all the meat is completely covered. Cook on medium low heat for 2 to 2 ½ hours stirring occasionally.

Serve over cooked spaghetti (or pasta of your choice) and sprinkle with grated Parmesan and Romano cheese (if desired).

> "This is the type of food I grew up with. Being Italian, my Mother would cook like this and my brothers and I would all sit around and eat together. Now my wife Keisha makes this dish— it's comfort food."
>
> –BILLY CONIGLIARO, BOSTON RED SOX 1969-1971
> 1973 WORLD CHAMPION OAKLAND A'S
> HOMETOWN: REVERE, MA

"*I like to make this dish when I have the time. It makes a large portion and makes the kitchen smell great. Food is always the way to a man's heart*"

—KEISHA CONIGLIARO

CHRIS MCCARRON'S
Savory Pork Chops

INGREDIENTS

6   *boneless pork chops*
(you can substitute **chicken**)

1   *cup* **butter** *(melted)*

2   *cups* **Kellogg's Corn Flakes**
(crushed)

1½ *cups of grated*
Parmesan cheese

1   *teaspoon* **garlic powder**

 Preheat the oven to 350°.

In a shallow bowl combine the Corn Flake crumbs, Parmesan cheese and garlic powder.

Melt the butter in a small saucepan over a low heat.

With a basting brush, spread the melted butter over a pork chop and then role in the crumb mixture. Repeat this step for all the pork chops.

Place all the pork chops in a baking dish and sprinkle the remaining crumb mixture over the top.

Pour the remaining butter over the top of the baking dish and bake for 50 to 60 minutes.

MAKES **6** **SERVINGS**

> "*What I like about this recipe is that it is so easy, tastes great and you can adjust the quantities depending on how many you are serving. The Corn Flakes make this dish really savory and give it something extra.*"
>
> –CHRIS MCCARRON, JOCKEY 1977-2005
> NATIONAL THOROUGHBRED HORSE RACING HALL OF FAME 1989
> HOMETOWN: BOSTON, MA

PATRICK PASS
Tangy Smoked Ribs

½   cup light **brown sugar**

½   cup **paprika**

1   tablespoon **black pepper**

1   tablespoon **chili powder**

1   tablespoon **garlic powder**

1   tablespoon **lemon pepper seasoning**

1   tablespoon crushed **rosemary**

1   tablespoon **Lawry's season salt**

2   racks of *St. Louis style baby back ribs*

1   cup **barbeque sauce** (we used **Sweet Baby Ray's**)

1   cup **ketchup**

½   cup **mustard**

1   tablespoon **Worcheshire sauce**

1   tablespoon **apple cider vinegar**

¼   cup **apple juice**

MAKES **6** SERVINGS

🏈 Remove the membrane from the back of the ribs (pull it away from the bone).

🏈 In a mixing bowl stir together the brown sugar, paprika, black pepper, chili powder, garlic powder, lemon pepper seasoning, rosemary and Lawry's season salt.

🏈 Coat the mixture all over the front and back of the ribs. Allow to marinate for at least 2 hours (you can marinate in the refrigerator for up to 24 hours).

🏈 When you are ready to cook, combine the barbeque sauce, ketchup, mustard, Worcheshire sauce, apple cider vinegar and apple juice in a saucepan over low heat for 5 to 7 minutes. Remove from heat and set aside.

🏈 Heat your smoker to about 250° to 300° and smoke the ribs until golden brown (3 to 4 hours). Every 30 minutes baste the ribs with the liquid mixture.

🏈 After the ribs are golden brown wrap them with aluminum foil for another 1.5 hours.

🏈 Let sit for 5 minutes, cut and serve.

> "*Being raised by a single Mom and my aunties in Georgia taught me about cooking and gave me an appreciation of southern recipes and flavors. I absolutely love to cook and this is one recipe I do all the time. The meat is very tender and the smoky flavor is fantastic.*"
>
> **–PATRICK PASS, NEW ENGLAND PATRIOTS 2000-2006**

> "*The goal is to teach kids more than just football skills. We want them to understand the value of teamwork and leadership and be able to apply those qualities to their everyday lives.*"
>
> —PATRICK
> @PPASS35

JOHNNY HAS BEEN PART OF THE BOSTON BRUINS FAMILY FOR 60 YEARS. WHILE PLAYING FOR THE BRUINS HE HELPED THEM WIN TWO STANLEY CUPS (1970 AND 1972). IN 2011, HIS NAME WAS ENGRAVED ON THE STANLEY CUP FOR A THIRD TIME.

JOHNNY BUCYK'S
The "Chief's" Easy Lemon Chicken

INGREDIENTS

4	whole **chicken breasts**
½	cup **butter** (melted)
½	teaspoon **thyme**
2	**lemons** (sliced thin)
	Salt
	Pepper
	Red pepper flakes (optional)

MAKES **8 SERVINGS**

- Preheat the oven to 350°

- Halve the chicken breasts and place in shallow 9x13 inch baking pan.

- Season with salt, pepper, thyme (and red pepper flakes, if desired).

- Pour melted butter over the chicken and arrange lemon slices on top of chicken pieces.

- Bake uncovered for an hour.

- Garnish with lemon slices.

> "I love chicken and this recipe is something that is quick and easy to do. This is a dish you can increase or decrease depending on how many people you need to feed."
>
> **–JOHNNY BUCYK, BOSTON BRUINS 1957-1978**
> **HOCKEY HALL OF FAME 1981**

MIKE ERUZIONE'S
Gold Medal Swordfish

INGREDIENTS

1   8 ounce **swordfish steak**

3-4 **bay scallops**

2   tablespoons **Old Bay seasoning**

3   tablespoons **olive oil**

½   teaspoon **salt**

½   teaspoon **pepper**

MAKES **1** SERVING

- Preheat the oven to 350°.

- In an oven-proof saucepan heat the olive oil on the stove over medium heat until hot.

- For the scallops: Coat with flour, Old Bay seasoning, salt and pepper.

- For the scallops: Add to the saucepan and sear on both sides for 2 to 3 minutes until cooked, remove and set aside.

- For the swordfish: Coat with Old Bay seasoning, salt and pepper. Add to the saucepan and sear on both sides for 2 to 3 minutes, place the saucepan in the oven and cook for 6 to 7 minutes until done.

- Plate the swordfish with the scallops and serve.

> "*I usually grill a lot for my family, but this is one of the few recipes I make for myself in the kitchen. It always comes out consistently good. Often times I eat the scallops as sort of an appetizer and the swordfish as the main meal.*"
>
> **—MIKE ERUZIONE, OLYMPIC HOCKEY PLAYER, GOLD MEDAL 1980**
> **HOMETOWN: WINTHROP, MA**

"*I've been very fortunate in my life. I try to spend my time focused on family—my own family, the Winthrop community that I consider family and my larger hockey family. It's important for me to give back to all those and do as much as I can.*"

—MIKE
@MERUZIONE

DREW NOW OWNS
DOUBLEBACK WINERY
WHICH ALLOWS HIM TO
COMBINE HIS PASSION
FOR FINE WINE WITH HIS
LOVE OF THE WALLA WALLA
VALLEY (HIS HOMETOWN).

"*Our goal is to
produce a world-
class Cabernet
Sauvignon.*"

THE 2007 CABERNET
SAUVIGNON, HAS RECEIVED
NUMEROUS ACCOLADES
EARNING A SPOT ON WINE
SPECTATOR'S TOP 100 LIST.

–DREW
WWW.DOUBLEBACK.COM

DREW BLEDSOE'S
Prime Rib with Homemade Horseradish Sauce

INGREDIENTS

For the prime rib

3-6 *pound* **prime rib**

1 *tablespoon* **salt**

1 *tablespoon* **pepper**

For the homemade horseradish sauce

½ *cup* **whipping cream**

½ *cup of* **mayonnaise**

1 *tablespoon* **horseradish**

1 *tablespoon* **dry mustard**

MAKES **6-8** SERVINGS

- Preheat the oven to 375°.
- Cover the entire prime rib with salt and pepper (to taste).
- Place the roast in a pan and put in the oven for 1 hour. After 1 hour immediately turn off the heat—DO NOT OPEN THE OVEN DOOR.
- Prior to serving turn the oven back on to 300°. For rare cook 45 minutes; for medium cook 50 minutes; for well-done cook 55 minutes. Cover with tin foil and let sit for 20 to 25 minutes before serving.
- For the homemade horseradish sauce: Using a mixer, mix the whipping cream on high for 3 to 4 minutes. Place the cream in the freezer for 10 minutes. Add the mayonnaise, horseradish and dry mustard and mix for another 2 minutes. Keep refrigerated before serving.
- Serve the prime rib with the horseradish sauce.
- Recommended wine pairing: Doubleback Cabernet Sauvignon™.

> **"The secret to this prime rib is it should be uncovered the whole time it is cooking. You can start this in the morning and then finish the last step before eating. My family makes this recipe every Christmas Eve and it turns out perfect every time."**
>
> **—DREW BLEDSOE, NEW ENGLAND PATRIOTS 1993-2001**

IN 2017, BOBBY RAN THE BOSTON MARATHON THE SECOND TIME PUSHING DENNA LAING IN A SPECIAL RACING WHEELCHAIR TO RAISE MONEY FOR JOURNEY FORWARD. HE IS NOW A COACH FOR THE KUNLUN RED STAR BASED IN BEIJING, CHINA. DAUGHTER ALEXANDRA IS PART OF THE US WOMEN'S OLYMPIC HOCKEY TEAM, SON BOBO PLAYS HOCKEY FOR BOSTON UNIVERSITY AND SON BRENDAN IS AWAY AT COLLEGE PLAYING FOOTBALL.

"It's a very crazy and hectic schedule but I wouldn't have it any other way."

—BOBBY
(JOURNEY-FORWARD.ORG)

BOBBY CARPENTER'S
Chicken Marsala

NGREDIENTS

2	**chicken breasts** (boneless, skinless and halved)
3	cups **baby bella mushrooms** (sliced)
6	tablespoons **butter**
¾	cup **flour**
¾	cup **Marsala wine**
½	cup **light cream**
½	cup **Carpenter's special seasoning** (even amounts of **garlic powder, onion powder, salt** and **pepper**)
2	tablespoons **olive oil**
2	tablespoons **cornstarch**
¾	pound **pasta** (your choice, cooked)

MAKES **4** SERVINGS

> "Since I was on my own a lot because of hockey, I had to learn to cook at an early age and my parents worked. Now, we spend a great deal of family time cooking. This is one of my favorite recipes, you can make this the exact same way with veal too."
>
> **–BOBBY CARPENTER**
> **BOSTON BRUINS 1988-1993,**
> **HOMETOWN: PEABODY, MA**

Using a large skillet melt 4 tablespoons of butter and sauté the mushrooms and 1 tablespoon of Carpenter's special seasoning over medium heat for 5 minutes. Remove the mushrooms and set aside.

In a plastic bag place the flour and one at a time place each chicken breast in it and shake until coated.

Using the same skillet, heat the olive oil, add the chicken and sprinkle with the remaining Carpenter's seasoning and sauté over medium heat for 8 minutes (turn after 4 minutes).

Add the mushrooms, cream, Marsala wine and remaining butter. Stir until combined and cook for 5 to 7 minutes.

Remove a ½ cup of the liquid from the skillet and place it in a cup or container.

Add the cornstarch to the liquid and mix together until smooth (this will make a roux which will thicken the sauce). Do not add the cornstarch directly to the skillet.

Pour the roux into the skillet and cook an additional 5 to 10 minutes until you get the sauce to your desired color and consistency. (Allow some of the liquid to burn off).

Pour over the cooked noodles of your choice. Let sit for 5 minutes and serve.

JEROD IS EXTREMELY BUSY. IN ADDITION TO BEING A DEVOTED HUSBAND AND FATHER OF THREE ACTIVE KIDS, HE IS BUSY WORKING AT OPTUM, SERVING ON THE BOARD OF TRUSTEES AT BOSTON MEDICAL CENTER AND HOSTING QUICK SLANTS ON NBC SPORTS BOSTON. HE IS VERY INVOLVED IN MANY CHARITABLE EFFORTS AND EVENTS, INCLUDING MAYO BOWL, WHICH BENEFITS BOSTON MEDICAL CENTER.

—@JEROD_MAYO51

JEROD MAYO
Chantel's Pelau

INGREDIENTS

3   pounds mixed **chicken pieces**
     (cut up bone-in, skin on)

2   tablespoons **Adobo seasoning**

1   tablespoon **Lawry's Season Salt**

2-3 teaspoons **black pepper**

1   tablespoon **Gravy Master**

3   tablespoons **Goya Mojo Criollo**

2   cans **pigeon peas**
     (30 to 32 ounces, drained)

MAKES 6-8 SERVINGS

> "*This is sort of an island-inspired dish. My wife Chantel is from Trinidad and this is one of our favorites. It's relatively healthy, it's fast and you can do it all in one pot. But the most important thing about this dish is that all my kids will eat it.*"
>
> **–JEROD MAYO, NEW ENGLAND PATRIOTS**
> **2008-2015**

🏈 In a bowl add the chicken, Adobo seasoning, Lawry's Season Salt, black pepper, Gravy Master and Goya Mojo Criollo. Combine all ingredients so the chicken is fully coated.

🏈 Let the chicken marinate for at least 20 minutes (you can marinate the chicken for up to a day in the refrigerator).

🏈 In a large deep skillet or Dutch Oven heat the olive oil over medium-high heat for 2 minutes.

🏈 Add the chicken, one piece at a time and pour the remaining marinade over the top. Cover the pot and allow the chicken to cook for 10 minutes (after 5 minutes turn the chicken so each side can get brown).

🏈 After 10 minutes, turn the heat on high for 3 to 5 minutes so the chicken can get completely brown.

🏈 Turn the heat down to simmer and add 2 cups of water. Add the rice and the squash, cover the pot and simmer for 20 to 25 minutes. (Check the mixture from time to time and if all the water is absorbed, slowly add more ¼ cup at a time).

🏈 Add the peas and cover again for 10 minutes. (Again, continually check to see if the pot needs more water and is your desired consistency). Remove from the heat.

🏈 Garnish each plate with avocado slices and serve.

"Years ago I put out a cookbook called 'Fowl Tips' which was a collection of chicken recipes because I had to be creative with having chicken for Wade four or five times a week."

—DEBBIE BOGGS

WADE BOGGS'
Chicken and Yellow Rice

INGREDIENTS

2-3 *pounds of **chicken** (breast, leg quarters skin on and bone-in)*

1 *medium **white onion** (peeled and chopped)*

2 *cloves **garlic** (finely chopped)*

1 ***bay leaf***

1 *envelope **Vigo flavor** and **coloring***

4 *ounces **pimentos***

6 *ounces **olive oil***

1 *can **green peas***

2 *teaspoons **garlic salt***

2 *medium **tomatoes** (cored and peeled)*

½ ***green bell pepper** (chopped)*

1 *pound **long grain rice***

2½ *cups **water***

MAKES **4-5** SERVINGS

☺ Heat 3 ounces of the olive oil in a skillet until hot. Add the chicken pieces with garlic salt and brown on both sides and set aside.

☺ In large skillet, heat 3 ounces of olive oil. Sauté the onion, garlic and green bell pepper. Add the tomatoes and simmer until soft. Add water, Vigo coloring, bay leaf and garlic salt and stir well to combine the flavors.

☺ Add in the chicken and bring everything to a boil. Reduce the heat and put lid on the skillet and simmer for 10 minutes.

☺ Bring the skillet to a boil again and stir in the rice. Boil together for 1 minute.

☺ Cover tightly and simmer for 25 to 30 minutes (check on the mixture at about the 15 minutes mark and add additional water for the rice, if necessary, to obtain your desired consistency).

☺ Remove the bay leaf and serve.

> **"Not only did I eat chicken before every game while I was playing, I still love eating chicken now. This is one of my favorites, the flavors are great together and it's fairly healthy."**
> –WADE BOGGS, BOSTON RED SOX 1982-1992
> BASEBALL HALL OF FAME 2005

CHRISTIAN AND WIFE KIM ARE EXTREMELY BUSY. HE IS THE HOST OF A WEEKDAY RADIO SHOW ON WEEI (ORWAY, MERLONI AND FAURIA) AND IS ALSO A FOOTBALL ANALYST. KIM IS THE CEO OF KJ DESIGNS AND CONSULTING AND IS A BUSY MOM BUT THEY TRY AS MUCH AS POSSIBLE TO BOND WITH THEIR CHILDREN OVER FOOD.

"*We try and sit down as a family for dinner at least three nights a week.*"

—KIM FAURIA, KJ DESIGNS
@KIMFAURIA
@CHRISTIANFAURIA

CHRISTIAN FAURIA
Kim's Eggplant Parmesan

INGREDIENTS

9-10 cups of pureed **red sauce**: *(homemade or your favorite jarred sauce, just make sure it is a puree without heavy chunks of tomato)*

3 medium **eggplants** *(sliced into thin rounds)*

4-5 cups of plain **bread crumbs**

4-5 large **eggs** *(lightly beaten)*

½ cup **all-purpose flour**

4 cups **vegetable oil**

1 pound **mozzarella cheese** *(sliced)*

2½ cups of shredded **Parmesan cheese**

1 teaspoon **salt**

1 teaspoon **garlic powder**

Coarse kosher salt

Pepper

MAKES 8-10 SERVINGS

> **"My wife made this recipe when we were first dating. She wanted to show me that good Italian food doesn't come frozen in a box like I was used to. What I like about it is that it is really authentic since it is made from scratch. It is truly the best eggplant parmesan ever."**
>
> **–CHRISTIAN FAURIA**
> **NEW ENGLAND PATRIOTS 2002-2005**

● Preheat the oven to 375°.

● Once the eggplants have been sliced into small circles (thin is the key here), start to warm up the oil in a fry pan over medium-low heat (heat up the oil slowly and then turn it up to medium-high about 5 minutes before you are ready to start frying the eggplant).

● In a small bowl make an egg wash: Beat the eggs with the salt, garlic powder and a pinch of pepper.

● Coat the eggplant using these steps: Dip each slice in the flour, the egg wash and finally the bread crumbs. Set them aside on a plate. Repeat this process for all the eggplant.

● Once all the eggplant is breaded, fry them in the oil until golden brown (crispy around the edges). Let them drain (to rid them of any excess oil) on a plate covered with a paper towel.

● While the eggplant is hot, salt the eggplant with the coarse kosher salt.

● Using a 9x13 inch baking pan start to layer by placing a thin layer of sauce on the bottom of the pan. Layer the eggplant over-lapping a bit so that none of the pan is visible. Next, layer with slices of mozzarella cheese (completely cover the eggplant). Place a thin layer of sauce on top of the cheese.

● Repeat these steps until you are almost at the top of the pan (finish with a layer of sauce). Before placing in the oven sprinkle the top with the parmesan cheese.

● Bake in the oven for 45 minutes and let sit for 15 minutes before serving. Serve with your favorite pasta and top with some extra sauce (if desired).

DICK IS DEDICATED TO THE HOYT FOUNDATION.

"*This foundation aspires to build the individual character, self-confidence and self-esteem of America's disabled young people through inclusion in all facets of their daily life– family, community activities and sports whether it's home, school or in the workplace.*"

—DICK (WWW.TEAMHOYT.COM)

DICK HOYT'S
Nutritious Salmon and Spinach

INGREDIENTS

For the salmon and spinach

2   **salmon filets** *(6 to 7 ounces each)*

3   tablespoons **olive oil**

3   tablespoons **lemon juice**

1   *10 ounce package* **fresh spinach** *(washed and dried)*

2   teaspoon **minced garlic**

For the yogurt topping

2   cups **Greek yogurt**

2   tablespoons **dill**

Salt

Pepper

MAKES (2) **SERVINGS**

Preheat the oven to 350°.

Coat the salmon filets with 1 tablespoon of the olive oil, 1 tablespoon lemon juice and sprinkle with salt and pepper (to taste). Place in the oven for 12 to 14 minutes.

In a large skillet heat 2 tablespoons of olive oil over medium heat. Add the spinach and cover for about 5 minutes. Add 2 table-spoons lemon juice, the minced garlic, salt and pepper (to taste). Cover again and cook for another 3 minutes.

In a small bowl combine the Greek yogurt, chopped mint, salt and pepper (to taste).

Lay the spinach on a platter and place the cooked salmon over it.

Garnish with the yogurt topping and sprinkle chopped mint or parsley (if desired).

> **"It's extremely important to eat healthy, it's one of the things that has helped us get through countless events including the Boston Marathon 32 times. Salmon is definitely one of my favorites."**
>
> **–DICK HOYT, BOSTON MARATHON RUNNER**
> **HOMETOWN: HOLLAND, MA**

JANE BLALOCK'S
Rack of Lamb

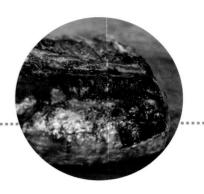

INGREDIENTS

8	rib **rack of lamb** (with the fat trimmed)
4	tablespoons **olive oil**
2	tablespoons **soy sauce**
2-3	tablespoons **Dijon mustard** (we used Nance's Sharp & Creamy)
2	teaspoon cracked **black pepper**
1	**garlic clove** (crushed)
1	tablespoon **parsley** (chopped)

MAKES **4** SERVINGS

⬤ To make the marinade, combine the olive oil, soy sauce, Dijon mustard, pepper, garlic and parsley in a bowl.

⬤ Let the ingredients sit for an hour (you can leave it out or refrigerate it).

⬤ Coat the rack of lamb on both sides with the marinade.

⬤ Broil the lamb on each side for 5 minutes.

⬤ After broiling, bake in the oven for 8 minutes at 400°.

⬤ Let the lamb sit for 3 to 5 minutes, carve and serve.

> "I enjoy lamb and what I really like about this recipe is that it comes out perfect each and every time. It doesn't take a long time to make and the marinade really brings out the flavor of the lamb. I make this frequently for family and friends when they come to visit."
>
> **–JANE BLALOCK, LGPA GOLFER**
> **HOMETOWN: PORTSMOUTH, NH**

JANE NOW OPERATES JBC GOLF WHICH RUNS GOLF CLINICS FOR WOMEN AND WAS INSTRUMENTAL IN STARTING THE WOMEN'S SENIOR GOLF TOUR (NOW THE LEGENDS TOUR). THE TOUR HAS DONATED A SIGNIFICANT AMOUNT OF MONEY TO VARIOUS CHARITIES OVER THE YEARS.

"*I like being involved in the game and teaching. I believe that empowering women on the golf course gives them confidence in all aspects of their lives.*"

— JANE @BLALOCKJANE

"*When I was growing up, everything was made with fresh, healthy, whole food. My grandpa was well ahead of his time. The only problem (if one can call it a problem) is that we don't use recipes. So please approach this 'recipe' with the 'a little of this, a little of that' mentality.*"

—JODY BUCKNER
BILLBUCKNER.NET

BILL BUCKNER'S
Rosemary Loin Lamb Chops over Wilted Spinach

INGREDIENTS

For the lamb chops

6   loin **lamb chops**

¾   cup **olive oil**

2   cloves **fresh garlic** *(finely chopped)*

½   cup dried **rosemary**

2   drops **hot pepper sauce**

     salt

     pepper

For the spinach

1   large bag **fresh baby spinach** *(washed)*

½   wedge **blue cheese** *(crumbled)*

2   tablespoons **olive oil**

     salt

     pepper

⚾ Mix the olive oil, finely chopped garlic, dried rosemary, salt and pepper (to taste) in a bowl. Marinate the lamb chops overnight in either a covered glass container or Ziploc bag.

⚾ On a hot grill, grill the lamb chops 3 minutes per side or to desired preference.

⚾ In a large skillet, heat the olive oil (about 2 minutes), add the spinach and salt and pepper (to taste). When the spinach is cooked (about 3-4 minutes) and wilted, add the blue cheese crumbles and stir.

⚾ Place the wilted blue cheese spinach on a platter and place grilled lamb chops on top.

MAKES **3** SERVINGS

> "What I like about this recipe is that it is quick and flavorful. My wide Jody comes from an Italian family of excellent cooks and this is her recipe. Enjoy!"
>
> **–BILL BUCKNER, BOSTON RED SOX 1984-1987**

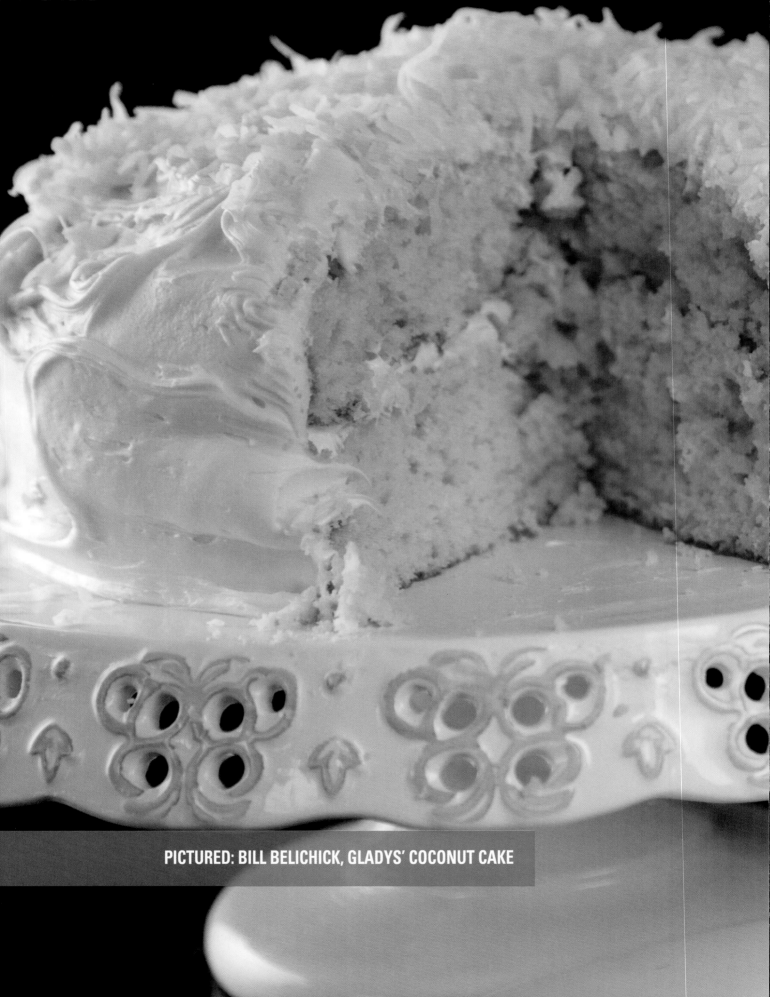

PICTURED: BILL BELICHICK, GLADYS' COCONUT CAKE

Desserts

THE COCHRAN FAMILY'S
Best Ever Cake

INGREDIENTS

1	tablespoon	**vinegar**
1	cup	**milk**
1	cup	**vegetable oil**
2	cups	**sugar**
½	cup	**cocoa**
1	cup	**water**
2½	cups	**flour**
2	teaspoon	**baking soda**
½	teaspoon	**salt**

MAKES (8) **SERVINGS**

◯◯◯ Preheat the oven to 350°.

◯◯◯ Add vinegar to milk (or use sour milk or buttermilk) and set aside.

◯◯◯ Add the oil, sugar, cocoa, and water into a bowl and beat until well mixed.

◯◯◯ Place the flour, baking soda and salt into another bowl and stir together.

◯◯◯ Alternately add the milk and oil mixture to the dry ingredients, stirring well after adding each one.

◯◯◯ Grease and flour a Bundt pan.

◯◯◯ Pour the batter into the Bundt pan and bake for 40 to 45 minutes.

◯◯◯ Let cool and remove from the pan (be careful so the cake does not break).

◯◯◯ Decorate with icing of your choice.

> "We make this cake for every family member's birthday, so that's quite a lot of cakes. The recipe is from a neighbor of ours when we were children and has been in our family ever since. We are so happy to pass it down to future generations."
>
> —BARBARA ANN COCHRAN
> ALPINE SKIER, OLYMPIC GOLD MEDALIST 1972, HOMETOWN: RICHMOND, VT

BARBARA ANN AND HER THREE SIBLINGS MARILYN, BOB AND LINDY ARE ALL NATIONAL CHAMPION SKIERS AND PART OF THE FAMOUS "SKIING COCHRANS" OF VERMONT. THE FAMILY HAS NOW EXPANDED TO INCLUDE THE NEXT GENERATION OF SKIERS. THE FAMILY OWNS THE COCHRAN SKI AREA (RICHMOND, VT) AND BARBARA IS ALSO THE OWNER OF GOLDEN OPPORTUNITIES IN SPORTS.

(COCHRANSKIAREA.COM)

SINCE RETIRING TY HAS BEEN BUSY BOUNCING AROUND OPENING A SERIES OF TRAMPOLINE PARKS CALLED "LAUNCH".

"What I love about it is that Launch is really for people of all ages and abilities. It's a great workout and a ton of fun."

—TY
LAUNCHTRAMPOLINEPARK.COM

TY LAW'S
Peach Cobbler

INGREDIENTS

2   *sticks* **butter**

2   *bags sliced* **frozen peaches**
     (or 6 **green apples** *cored and cut*
     into sections)

2   *8 ounce cans* **crescent rolls**

1   *can* **lightly colored soda**
     (we used **Mountain Dew**)

½   *cup* **sugar**

1   *teaspoon* **vanilla**

MAKES (8) SERVINGS

> **"This recipe is one of my all-time favorite desserts. It is so gooey and delicious. I make this recipe using sliced apples too. It is a regular in the Law household"**
>
> **—TY LAW, NEW ENGLAND PATRIOTS**
> **1995-2004**

🏈 Preheat the oven to 350°.

🏈 Once the peaches have defrosted, roll 1 or 2 peaches (depending on the size) in each crescent roll and place in a well buttered 9X13 inch baking pan.

🏈 In a saucepan melt the butter on low heat and stir in the sugar and the vanilla (lightly stir together).

🏈 Pour the butter mixture over the top of the peaches and crescent rolls.

🏈 Pour the soda (about half the can) around the edges of the pan and sprinkle with 1 tablespoon of cinnamon.

🏈 Bake for 40 minutes and place some of the liquid in a saucepan.

🏈 Stir the liquid on medium until brown (about 2 to 3 minutes).

🏈 Pour over the top of the baking pan and sprinkle with remaining cinnamon.

🏈 Optional (shown here): Bake for 20 minutes. Remove from the oven and top with any remaining peaches.

🏈 Return to the oven for the remaining 20 minutes and continue with directions above.

🏈 Top with ice-cream of your choice before serving.

BILL IS THE ULTIMATE ROLE MODEL AND MENTOR AND FULLY BELIEVES IN THE MENTORING PROCESS. HIS INVOLVEMENT IN THE NATIONAL MENTORING PARTNERSHIP AND BILL RUSSELL MENTORING GRANT PROGRAM ENSURES THAT TODAY'S YOUTH WILL BE SURROUNDED BY AN ADULT WHO PROVIDES GUIDANCE AND SUPPORT.

"Today's children are everyone's responsibility."

–BILL
(WWW.MENTORING.ORG)
@REALBILLRUSSELL

BILL RUSSELL'S
Spanking Good Banana Pudding

INGREDIENTS

For the pudding

⅓ cup **sugar**
⅓ cup **cornstarch**
4 large **egg yolks**
2 cups **whole milk**
2 teaspoons **banana flavoring**
2 tablespoons of **salted butter**
3 **bananas** *(sliced into rounds)*
2 cups of **vanilla wafers**

For the whipped cream

2 cups cold heavy **whipping cream**
3 tablespoons **sugar**
1 teaspoon **vanilla extract**

> "*I still remember to this day every time my mom would make banana pudding I would get a spanking. As a child, my mom would make banana pudding and set it on the windowsill to cool. I could never resist and would always have to have a taste. I figured if I was going to get a spanking for one bite, I might as well make it worth my while and eat the entire bowl*".
>
> **–BILL RUSSELL**
> **BOSTON CELTICS 1956-1969**
> **HALL OF FAME 1975**

✺ With a hand mixer combine the egg yolks, cornstarch, sugar and butter and blend together in a large bowl until smooth.

✺ In a double-boiler, bring the milk to a slight boil and remove from the heat.

✺ Slowly whisk the milk into the bowl (make sure to keep stirring and not "cook" the eggs).

✺ Pour the mixture back into the double-boiler and add the banana flavoring. Continue to stir over medium heat until the mixture thickens (about 4 to 5 minutes).

✺ Once thickened, pour the mixture into a clean bowl and set aside to cool for 3 to 4 hours (to speed the process you can put this in the refrigerator for about 2 hours).

✺ For the whipped cream: Combine the heavy whipping cream, sugar and vanilla extract into a bowl and whip on high with a mixer until desired thickness, refrigerate until ready to use.

✺ To serve: Slice the bananas into rounds and line the bottom of a glass serving bowl (you can also make individual servings in a glass).

✺ Add some vanilla wafers and then some pudding. Repeat this process so that the bowl is layered. Top with whipped cream and serve.

MAKES 4-6 SERVINGS

DREW AND HIS WIFE CAROLYN ARE ALWAYS LOOKING FOR WAYS TO GIVE BACK.

"When you are in a position like we (athletes) are, its important try and to do as much as you can to help others."

—DREW
@DREWPOMERANZ
@CAROLYNESSERMAN

DREW POMERANZ'S
Baked S'mores

INGREDIENTS

1½ sticks **butter** *(melted)*

¾ cup **sugar**

2 **eggs**

½ cup **flour**

½ teaspoon **salt**

10 ounces **graham crackers** *(crushed)*

1½ teaspoons **baking powder**

2 cups **marshmallow fluff**

5 1.5 ounce **Hershey chocolate bars**

1 teaspoon **hot water**

½ cup **chocolate sauce** *(for garnish, if desired)*

MAKES  6-9 SERVINGS

⚾ Preheat the oven to 350.

⚾ In a large bowl mix together the eggs, butter, sugar, graham crackers, flour, salt and baking powder.

⚾ Using a 9x9 or 8x10 inch baking pan (greased), press half the graham cracker mixture across the bottom of the pan until it is covered.

⚾ Spread the chocolate bars across the pan evenly (make sure it covers the bottom layer).

⚾ In a mixing bowl, stir together the fluff and the water (the water will make it easier to spread). Spread over the top of the chocolate layer until covered.

⚾ Spread the rest of the graham cracker mixture over the top (it is fine if you see some of the marshmallow coming through).

⚾ Bake for 35 minutes.

⚾ Cool in the pan for 15 minutes before serving.

⚾ Top with chocolate sauce (if desired)

> **"This is my wife's Carolyn's recipe. It's is very rich but tastes great. No matter what the weather or where you live, it's a slice of summer all year round."**
> **–DREW POMERANZ, BOSTON RED SOX 2016-PRESENT**

IN 1986 SATCH FORMED THE ROOKIE TRANSITION PROGRAM FOR THE NBA. THE GOAL OF THE PROGRAM IS TO ALLOW ROOKIES TO TRANSITION SMOOTHLY INTO THE NBA AND THEIR TEAMS. SATCH STILL RESIDES IN NEW ENGLAND AND IS EXTREMELY INVOLVED IN THE LOCAL COMMUNITY.

"Passing on the lessons I've learned over the years to young people is a passion of mine."

—SATCH

TOM 'SATCH' SANDERS'
Fruited Sweet Potato Pie

INGREDIENTS

2	large **sweet potatoes**
⅓	cup **granulated sugar**
½	cup shredded **coconut flakes**
¼	teaspoon of **salt**
¼	teaspoon of **baking soda**
1	teaspoon powdered **cinnamon**
⅛	teaspoon grated **nutmeg**
⅛	teaspoon **powdered cloves**
6	tablespoons of **salted butter**
1	teaspoon **vanilla flavor**
1	**egg**
1	ounce **evaporated milk**
½	cup **white raisins**
1	**graham cracker pie crust**

MAKES 6 SERVINGS

✳ Rinse the potatoes, place in cold water and bring to a boil over medium-high heat.

✳ Boil until they are tender (35 to 45 minutes).

✳ Drain and allow potatoes to cool until they can be handled. Peel the potatoes, place in mixing bowl and mash.

✳ Preheat the oven to 375°.

✳ Add all ingredients (in order listed above) except for the white raisins.

✳ Mix on a low speed (or mash) until relatively smooth.

✳ Stir in the white raisins.

✳ Pour or spoon (depending on consistency) into the pie shell.

✳ Bake for 40 minutes. Cool and serve.

❝This sweet potato pie was a family favorite. I thoroughly enjoyed bringing this wonderful dessert to Boston when I opened Satch's Restaurant in the early 80's. The best part was having my mother make the pies that became one of our most popular menu items. I'm happy to share it with everyone.❞

–TOM "SATCH" SANDERS
BOSTON CELTICS 1960-1973, HALL OF FAME 2011

PAT BRADLEY'S
Champions' Delight

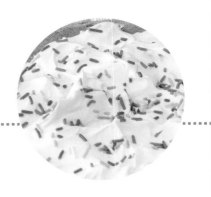

INGREDIENTS

1   6 pack **Hershey chocolate bars**
      (plain or with almonds)

2   8 ounce tubs **Cool Whip**

1   *graham cracker crust pie pan*

     Jimmies, sprinkles
     mini-chocolate chips
     (or your own toppings)

MAKES **6** SERVINGS

⊕ In a saucepan over medium heat, melt the chocolate bars, continually stirring with a wooden spoon or spatula (you can use a double boiler to make sure you do not boil or burn the chocolate).

⊕ Slowly add scoops of Cool Whip until it reaches your desired consistency (make sure to save some Cool Whip for the top).

⊕ Pour mixture into a graham cracker pie crust and place in refrigerator for 20 to 30 minutes to set.

⊕ Cover the top with remaining Cool Whip and decorate as desired.

> "*I always loved making this recipe when I won an event. It's really easy but yummy and it makes you feel like you are rewarding yourself for accomplishing something.*"
>
> **–PAT BRADLEY, LPGA GOLFER**
> **HALL OF FAME 1991**
> **HOMETOWN: WESTFORD, MA**

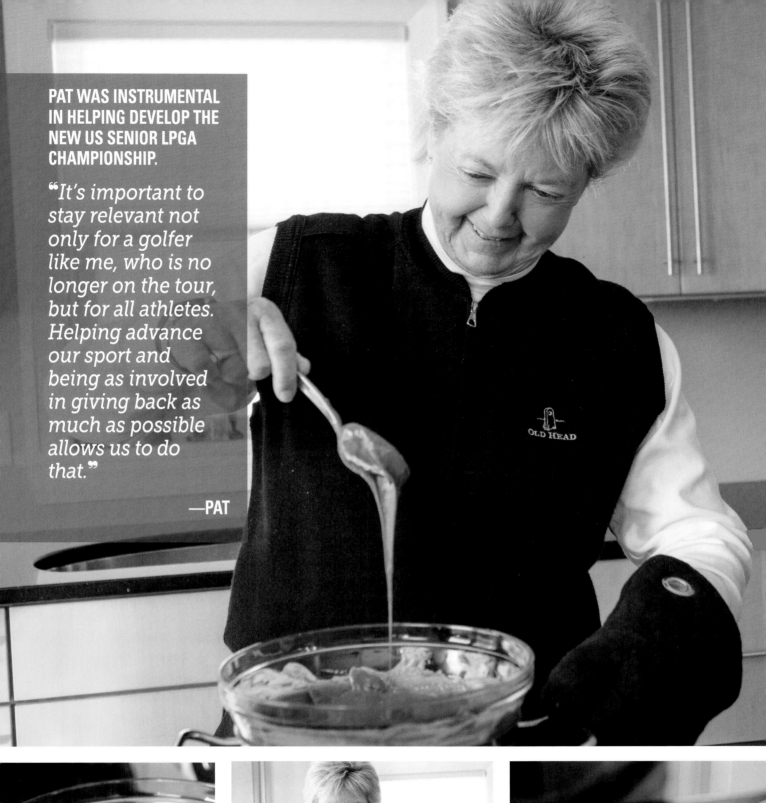

PAT WAS INSTRUMENTAL IN HELPING DEVELOP THE NEW US SENIOR LPGA CHAMPIONSHIP.

"*It's important to stay relevant not only for a golfer like me, who is no longer on the tour, but for all athletes. Helping advance our sport and being as involved in giving back as much as possible allows us to do that.*"

—PAT

"*This recipe is based on one from 'The Modern Cooking Guide' published in 1946. My grandmother, Gladys McAfee Greene, referred to this cookbook until the pages had been tattered and torn. She pretty much raised me as a young girl growing up in the deep south of Tennessee. Now I share this recipe with my daughters Kat and Ashley as well as the rest of my family. I hope you enjoy my family dessert recipe with your loved ones as much as we have with ours and the conversation that's inspired from it!*"

—LINDA HOLLIDAY

BILLBELICHICKFOUNDATION.ORG

BILL BELICHICK
Gladys' Coconut Cake

INGREDIENTS

4	*eggs*
1	*cup grated* **coconut**
1	*cup* **butter** *(softened)*
2	*teaspoons* **vanilla**
1	*teaspoon* **coconut flavoring**
3	*cups* **flour**
2	*cups* **sugar**
4	*teaspoons* **baking powder**
1	*teaspoon* **salt**
2	*cups* **water**

MAKES 8-10 SERVINGS

- Preheat the oven to 350°.

- Butter and flour two 9 x 9 inch cake pans.

- In a large bowl combine the eggs, butter, vanilla, coconut flavoring, flour, sugar, baking powder, salt and water using a mixer on medium speed.

- Once all the ingredients are combined and the batter is smooth, stir in the coconut and mix well.

- Pour half the batter into each cake pan and place into the oven.

- Bake for 35 to 40 minutes and let cool for 20 minutes.

- Frost and decorate as desired.

> **"I think that certain foods bring back memories and special events that have happened throughout our lives. This is Linda's grandmother's coconut cake and I have enjoyed this on numerous occasions."**
>
> **–BILL BELICHICK, NEW ENGLAND PATRIOTS COACH 2000-PRESENT**

TROY BROWN'S
Sweet Mini Cheesecake Bites

INGREDIENTS

2	cups **graham cracker crumbs**
1½	cups **butter** *(melted)*
1	teaspoon **cinnamon**
2	8 ounces packages **cream cheese**
¾	cup **sugar**
⅔	cup **sour cream**
1	**egg**
1	teaspoon **vanilla extract**
1	can **cherry pie filling**

🏈 Preheat the oven to 350°.

🏈 In a mixing bowl, stir together the graham cracker crumbs, butter, 1 ½ teaspoons sugar and cinnamon. Once combined, divide evenly and press into a non-stick mini muffin pan.

🏈 Using a mixer, on medium speed, mix the cream cheese with 2/3 cup of sugar. Slowly add 1 egg and vanilla. Once combined, mix in the sour cream. Fill mini-muffin each about a ¾ of the way full.

🏈 Bake for 20 minutes.

🏈 Let cool and refrigerate for 1 hour.

🏈 Top with 1 cherry pie filling per mini cheesecake.

MAKES **10** **SERVINGS**

> "I like the little bites because I can eat so many of them. I always like something sweet, even when I was playing I would eat ice-cream and cookies with a side of hot fudge before games."
>
> **–TROY BROWN**
> **NEW ENGLAND PATRIOTS, 1993-2007**

TROY IS CURRENTLY ON-AIR WITH NBC SPORTS BOSTON AND SPENDS MUCH OF HIS TIME WITH HIS FAMILY AND DOING CHARITY WORK.

"I know everyone knows about 'TB-12,' but I was the original TB-80. I think he [Tom Brady] might have stolen that from me."

—TROY @REALTROYBROWN80

BRAD AND TRACY STEVENS ARE INVOLVED WITH NUMEROUS CHARITY EFFORTS AND NONE IS MORE IMPORTANT TO THEM THAN THE AMERICAN CANCER SOCIETY'S COACHES VS. CANCER (NOW THE 2K SPORTS CLASSIC). THEY HAVE BEEN INVOLVED IN IT SINCE BRAD WAS COACHING AT BUTLER. IN 2004 TRACY'S MOTHER PASSED AWAY FROM THE DISEASE.

"When things like that happen, it really hits home."

—BRAD
@BCCOACHSTEVENS

BRAD STEVENS
Tracy's Chocolate Chocolate Chip Cupcakes

INGREDIENTS

1   box of **devil's food cake mix**

½   cup **vegetable oil**

1¼   cups **water**

6   ounces instant **chocolate pudding mix**

4   **eggs**

⅛   cup **sour cream**

12   ounces semisweet **chocolate chips**

MAKES 24 SERVINGS

✺ Preheat the oven to 350°.

✺ Using a mixer (on medium speed) combine the cake mix, pudding mix, eggs, water, oil and sour cream.

✺ Once the mixture is smooth, add the bag of chocolate chips and stir thorough.

✺ Bake in cupcake tins, filling each tin about two-thirds of the way full for 22 to 23 minutes.

✺ Let the cupcakes cool for at least 20 minutes then frost and decorate with icing and toppings of your choice.

> "We try and eat pretty healthy, so this is a little bit of a splurge. These cupcakes are so chocolaty and my wife Tracy tends to make them for birthdays or special celebration."
>
> **–BRAD STEVENS**
> **BOSTON CELTICS HEAD COACH 2013-PRESENT**

A

Allen, Ray, 101

B

Beckett, Josh, 39
Belichick, Bill, 213
Bird, Larry, 95
Blalock, Jane, 195
Bledsoe, Drew, 183
Boggs, Wade, 189
Bourque, Ray, 71
Bradley, Pat, 211
Brown, Alya, 115
Brown, Dee, 107
Brown, Troy, 109, 215
Buckner, Bill, 103, 197
Bucyk, Johnny, 91, 179

C

Carpenter, Bobby, 185
Caron, Tom, 55
Chatham, Matt, 59
Clayborn, Ray, 169
Clemens, Roger, 83
Cochran Family, 201
Conigliaro, Billy, 173
Cowens, Dave, 47
Craig, Jim, 137
Craven, Ricky, 61

D

DeOssie, Steve, 97, 129

E

Eruzione, Mike, 181

F

Fauria, Christian, 191
Faxon, Brad, 163
Ference, Andrew, 15
Flutie, Doug, 145
Francona, Terry, 63

G

Gomes, Jonny, 69
Grafton, Colin, 171
Green, Jarvis, 29, 123
Grogan, Steve, 37
Gronkowski, Rob, 77

H

Hanefeld, Kirk, 143
Havlicek, John, 121
Heaps, Jay, 25
Heinsohn, Tommy, 167
Hogan, Chris, 87
Hoyt, Dick, 193

J

Johnson, Ted, 85

K

Koppen, Dan, 79
Krug, Torey, 125

L
Lago, Scotty, 43
Lane, Max, 49
Law, Ty, 203
Light, Matt, 93, 133
Lobo, Rebecca, 157
Lynn, Fred, 159

M
Martinez, Pedro, 165
Maxwell, Cedric, 111, 141
McCarty, Walter, 113, 131
McCarron, Chris, 175
McKenney, Don, 17
Mayo, Jerod, 187
Moore, Charlie, 155
Morris, John, 75

N
Neely, Cam, 139

O
Ortiz, David, 51, 73, 149

P
Pac, Erin, 53
Pass, Patrick, 177
Paxton, Lonnie, 65
Paz, Vinny, 41
Pomeranz, Drew, 207

Q
Quinn (Sacramone), Alicia, 153

R
Ramirez, Manny, 127
Rask, Tuukka, 147
Rodgers, Bill, 27
Russell, Bill, 205

S
Sanders, Thomas "Satch", 209
Scalabrine, Brian, 135
Schmidt, Milt, 23
Shnapir, Simon, 35
Shoemaker, Jarrod, 19
Slater, Matthew, 99
Smerlas, Fred, 97, 129
Stevens, Brad, 217

T
Taygan, Ferdi, 117
Thornton, Shawn, 161
Tippett, Andre, 151

V
Vollmer, Sebastian, 105

Wakefield, Tim, 45
Werner, Tom, 31
Wiggins, Jermaine, 57

Y
Youkilis, Kevin, 81

my recipe notes

my recipe notes